LANGSTON HUGHES

A Study of the Short Fiction

Also available in Twayne's Studies in Short Fiction Series

Sherwood Anderson: A Study of the Short Fiction by Robert Allen Papinchak
Donald Barthelme: A Study of the Short Fiction by Barbara L. Roe
Samuel Beckett: A Study of the Short Fiction by Robert Cochran
Jorge Luis Borges: A Study of the Short Fiction by Naomi Lindstrom
Elizabeth Bowen: A Study of the Short Fiction by Phyllis Lassner
Kay Boyle: A Study of the Short Fiction by Elizabeth S. Bell
Truman Capote: A Study of the Short Fiction by Helen S. Garson
Raymond Carver: A Study of the Short Fiction by Ewing Campbell
Willa Cather: A Study of the Short Fiction by Loretta Wasserman
John Cheever: A Study of the Short Fiction by James O'Hara
Robert Coover: A Study of the Short Fiction by Thomas E. Kennedy
Stephen Crane: A Study of the Short Fiction by Chester Wolford
Andre Dubus: A Study of the Short Fiction by Thomas E. Kennedy
F. Scott Fitzgerald: A Study of the Short Fiction by John Kuehl
John Gardner: A Study of the Short Fiction by Jeff Henderson
William Goyen: A Study of the Short Fiction by Reginald Gibbons
Graham Greene: A Study of the Short Fiction by Richard Kelly
Ernest Hemingway: A Study of the Short Fiction by Joseph M. Flora
Henry James: A Study of the Short Fiction by Richard A. Hocks
Franz Kafka: A Study of the Short Fiction by Allen Thiher
Bernard Malamud: A Study of the Short Fiction by Robert Solotaroff
Katherine Mansfield: A Study of the Short Fiction by J. F. Kobler
Gabriel Garcia Márquez: A Study of the Short Fiction by Harley D. Oberhelman
Flannery O'Connor: A Study of the Short Fiction by Suzanne Morrow Paulson
Liam O'Flaherty: A Study of the Short Fiction by James M. Cahalan
Grace Paley: A Study of the Short Fiction by Neil D. Isaacs
Edgar Allan Poe: A Study of the Short Fiction by Charles E. May
V. S. Pritchett: A Study of the Short Fiction by John J. Stinson
J. D. Salinger: A Study of the Short Fiction by John Wenke
William Saroyan: A Study of the Short Fiction by Edward Halsey Foster
Irwin Shaw: A Study of the Short Fiction by James R. Giles
Isaac Bashevis Singer: A Study of the Short Fiction by Edward Alexander
John Steinbeck: A Study of the Short Fiction by R. S. Hughes
Peter Taylor: A Study of the Short Fiction by James Curry Robison
Robert Penn Warren: A Study of the Short Fiction by Joseph R. Millichap
Edith Wharton: A Study of the Short Fiction by Barbara A. White
Tennessee Williams: A Study of the Short Fiction by Dennis Vannatta
William Carlos Williams: A Study of the Short Fiction by Robert Gish
Virginia Woolf: A Study of the Short Fiction by Dean Baldwin

Twayne's Studies in Short Fiction

Gordon Weaver, General Editor
Oklahoma State University

LANGSTON HUGHES
Photograph courtesy of Amistad Research Center, Tulane University

LANGSTON HUGHES

_____ *A Study of the Short Fiction* ___

Hans Ostrom
University of Puget Sound

TWAYNE PUBLISHERS · *NEW YORK*
Maxwell Macmillan Canada · *Toronto*
Maxwell Macmillan International · *New York Oxford Singapore Sydney*

Twayne's Studies in Short Fiction Series, No. 47

Copyright © 1993 by Twayne Publishers

Twayne Publishers
Macmillan Publishing Company
866 Third Avenue
New York, New York 10022

Maxwell Macmillan Canada, Inc.
1200 Eglinton Avenue East
Suite 200
Don Mills, Ontario M3C 3N1

Library of Congress Cataloging-in-Publication Data

Ostrom, Hans A.
  Langston Hughes : a study of the short fiction / Hans Ostrom.
    p. cm. — (Twayne's studies in short fiction ; no. 47)
  Includes bibliographical references and index.
  ISBN 0-8057-8343-1
  1. Hughes, Langston, 1902–1967—Criticism and interpretation.
  2. Afro-Americans in literature. 3. Short story. I. Title.
  II. Series.
  PS3515.U274Z689 1993
  813'.52—dc20   93-18405
                                                                CIP

The paper used in this publication meets the minimum requirements of American National Standard for Information Sciences—Permanence of Paper for Printed Library Materials. ANSI Z3948-1984. ⊚™

10 9 8 7 6 5 4 3 2 1

Printed in the United States of America

Contents

Preface   xi
Acknowledgments   xiii

PART 1. THE SHORT FICTION

The Ways of White Folks   3
Laughing to Keep from Crying   19
*The Jesse B. Simple Stories
    and Something in Common*   31
Character Types and Narrative Modes   51
Epilogue   60
Notes to Part 1   64

PART 2. THE WRITER

Introduction   69
Notes to Part 2   79

PART 3. THE CRITICS

Introduction   83
Alain Locke   85
Arna Bontemps   86
Carl Van Vechten   87
Luther Jackson   88
Melvin Tolson   89
Arnold Rampersad   90
Onwuchekwa Jemie   91
R. Baxter Miller   92
Arthur P. Davis   93
Houston A. Baker, Jr.   94
Steven C. Tracy   95
Phyllis R. Klotman   96

Contents

Susan Blake   97
Edward Margolies   98
James O. Young   99
Mary Rohrberger   100
Jeffrey Walker   101
James Emanuel   102
Hoyt Fuller   103
Adam David Miller   104
Amiri Baraka   105
Notes to Part 3   106

Chronology   107
Bibliography   110
Index   119

Preface

Langston Hughes holds a fixed place in the literature of the United States, a place that seems to depend on his roles as "blues poet" and as one parent of the African-American literary aesthetic that matured in the 1960s and 1970s.

One problem with places and roles in a nation's literature, however, is that they can be reductive; often the career, the body of work, the complexity of the work are streamlined to fit into different versions of literary history. Scholars and critics can be hasty and shortsighted as they weave assessments of writers into narratives about epochs of literature.

So even if we believe it is fortunate and correct for Hughes to hold a secure place in the literature of the United States, we might also pay attention to how his achievement has been oversimplified. Even as a poet, for example, he is much more than a blues poet. Moreover, his contributions to drama, autobiography, and editing remain enormously influential but undervalued. So does his achievement in short fiction.

The standard apologia for a study of this sort is that the material in question—Hughes's short stories, in this case—has received insufficient attention. The case of Hughes does not, however, completely warrant such a claim. Critics have written a fair amount on Hughes's stories, and for the most part what they have written has treated the stories well; in this sense, the attention paid to the short fiction has been substantial.

Nonetheless, a few necessary pieces are missing in the body of criticism that explicitly concerns Hughes as a story writer. For example, aside from an unpublished doctoral dissertation in 1962, no one has undertaken a comprehensive study of the stories. More importantly, perhaps, a couple of circumstances have caused Hughes's achievement in short fiction to be underestimated.

The first is this: until fairly recently, scholars, critics, and reviewers have tended to associate African-American fiction almost exclusively with the novel, and more particularly with the novels of Claude McKay, Richard Wright, Ralph Ellison, James Baldwin, Toni Morrison, and Alice Walker, for instance. Because Hughes made only one real attempt to write a long fictional narrative, *Not Without Laughter* (1930), it became easy to identify him chiefly with his poetry and reflexively overlook what he achieved in fiction. But if one pauses to look at how many stories Hughes wrote, how originally he approached the genre, and especially how he wedded social critique to the art of the short narrative, a marvelous new dimension of his career becomes more visible.

The second circumstance producing a chronic underestimation of his fiction lies, ironically, in one of Hughes's most remarkable achievements in the form: the creation of Jesse B. Simple, urban folk hero. Reading only a couple of the Simple stories or reading only *about* Simple in an anthology headnote, for instance, can lead to a condescending or dismissive attitude toward this extraordinary character, who is much more than a comic, fictional citizen of Harlem at midcentury. A consideration of Hughes's sustained achievement with Simple reveals the character to be as complex, supple, and original as that other famous American wise fool, Huckleberry Finn. Moreover, the short narratives Hughes crafted around Simple are virtually unique in their blend of folk, belles lettres, vaudevillian, blues, journalistic, and satiric techniques. But almost like a Zen painter—or a blues musician—Hughes disguised the complex techniques required to produce such spare but sophisticated stories. Consequently, one task of this study is to illuminate Hughes's achievement in the Simple stories.

This book, then, is not intended somehow to rescue Hughes's reputation, which is secure, but to carefully reevaluate the body of his work in short fiction; to determine how Hughes implicitly defined the short story for himself and others; and to offer both close readings and synthesizing interpretations of stories Hughes published in five different decades.

The study is also intended to reveal a certain ethnographic impulse in his short fiction: Hughes's steadfast desire to provide a fictional thick description of American society and particularly of working-class African-Americans. In this regard, Hughes is a compatriot of Zora Neal Hurston; Hurston's own remarkable achievement in short fiction has been rediscovered and celebrated in recent years, a circumstance that makes this reconsideration of Hughes's stories even more timely and appropriate.

The chief organizing principle of part 1, which analyzes and assesses the stories, is roughly chronological, starting with the first collection (*The Ways of White Folks*), working through *Laughing to Keep from Crying* and the Simple stories (which are collected in several volumes), and ending with what amounted to Hughes's "selected stories": *Something in Common* (1963). I also provide—in chapter 4–an interpretive cross section that examines certain character types and recurring narrative modes. Chapter 5, which functions as an epilogue, discusses key ironies and paradoxes inherent in Hughes's writing and his career—ironies and paradoxes for which his short fiction serves as an especially useful focusing lens.

Throughout part 1, I rely on a variety of critical methods. Among them are reader-response and genre criticism; literary history; and the enormously instructive, relatively new multicultural approaches of Houston Baker, Henry Louis Gates, Jr., and other critics who continue to illuminate African-American literary traditions in powerful ways.

Part 2 provides a sense of Hughes's own ideas about his career, the writing life, and the unique predicaments of African-American writers—chiefly as these ideas bear on his short fiction. This part of the book begins by quoting from and discussing Hughes's most important piece of literary criticism, "The Negro Artist and the Racial Mountain" (1926), and then draws on a variety of speeches, essays, and works of autobiography. Although several interviews with Hughes were published, none proved to be particularly helpful in shedding light on Hughes as a story writer. Moreover, Hughes was generally an extremely diffident interviewee.

Part 3 surveys reviews, articles, and assessments within books of specific Hughes stories and his overall achievement in short fiction. The survey is intended to be representative, not exhaustive.

Depending upon the context, I use the terms "Negro," "black," and "African-American" at different times in this book, not to create confusion but to recognize and respect the ways in which terminology must necessarily change over time and in different rhetorical situations.

The bibliography provides a generous but by no means complete representation of Hughes's own work and of criticism and scholarship on Hughes, particularly as such secondary sources relate to his short fiction. One slight difference between this bibliography and the others in *Twayne's Studies in Short Ficton* series is that it lists Hughes's many produced but unpublished plays which may interest scholars investigating Hughes's drama in particular or African-American theatre in general.

Acknowledgments

I am grateful for permission to quote from the following works:

Laughing to Keep From Crying by Langston Hughes, copyright © 1952, by Langston Hughes. Copyright © renewed 1980 by George Houston Bass.

The Langston Hughes Reader by Langston Hughes, copyright © 1958 by Langston Hughes. Copyright © renewed 1986 by George Houston Bass.

Simple Speaks His Mind by Langston Hughes, copyright © 1950 by Langston Hughes. Copyright © renewed 1978 by George Houston Bass.

"The Negro Artist and the Racial Mountain" by Langston Hughes, *The Nation*. Copyright © 1926 by Langston Hughes.

The Ways of White Folks by Langston Hughes, copyright © 1934 by Alfred A. Knopf.

The Big Sea, I Wonder As I Wander, The Best of Simple, Simple's Uncle Sam by Langston Hughes, copyright © Hill & Wang/Farrar, Straus, & Giroux.

The Big Sea by Langston Hughes, copyright © Langston Hughes 1940. Published in Britain by Pluto Press.

The Life of Langston Hughes by Arnold Rampersad (2 volumes), copyright © 1986 and 1988 by Oxford University Press.

Photograph of Langston Hughes courtesy of the Countee Cullen Papers, The Amistand Research Center, Tulane University.

I am very grateful to my editor at Twayne, Melissa Solomon and to my copy editor, 'Annah Sobelman. My colleague at the University of Puget Sound, Professor William Lyne, has enhanced my understanding of Langston Hughes. Professor Arnold Rampersad of Princeton University provided generous advice at a crucial moment in the project. Ronald Keyes and Sharon Kernal were most helpful in identifying Hughes material in the special collections at Langston University, Langston, Oklahoma. Thanks are also due to Andrew Simons, Reference Archivist at the Amistad Research Center at Tulane University, and the library staff at the University of Puget Sound. Professor Gordon Weaver, the field editor, provided excellent advice throughout the course of the project. I am grateful to Jane Kendall and Craig Smart for their help. And Jacquelyn Bacon Ostrom has offered constant and insightful support of my work in general and of this book in particular.

Part 1

THE SHORT FICTION

The Ways of White Folks

Overview: The Genesis and Achievement of *The Ways of White Folks*

One important preliminary observation to make about *The Ways of White Folks* (1934) is that although it is Hughes's first collection of stories, it is not the work of an inexperienced writer. Hughes had written and published poetry extensively, established a literary reputation within the Harlem Renaissance, and traveled throughout the United States and the world at a feverish pace.

Moreover, many of his aesthetic and political ideas had matured; he knew what he wanted his short story to look like and the kind of worldview he wanted it to reflect. His landmark essay, "The Negro Artist and the Racial Mountain," which amounted to a literary/political manifesto for himself and others of his generation, had appeared in 1926.

The Ways of White Folks, which appeared after an extensive process of artistic and personal development, possesses a unity and force of vision uncommon to first collections. Consequently, the book remains an important point on the map of American short fiction, comparable to Sherwood Anderson's *Winesburg, Ohio*, Katherine Anne Porter's *Flowering Judas*, and Ernest Hemingway's *In Our Time*. Even after several decades of scrutiny, it is among the few first collections that do not seem mannered, quaint, thin, or otherwise severely limited.

As this chapter and part 3 discuss, however, the collection has not engendered uniform critical praise, largely because it addresses questions of racial, class, and sexual conflict so directly, uses fierce, even bitter, irony, and reflects Hughes's notions about short fiction, which were not altogether mainstream. The critical resistance the collection has encountered, however, is in a sense only another measure of the book's distinctiveness.

Placed in an international context of short fiction, Hughes's first collection is comparable to James Joyce's *Dubliners*—at least in the way it presents an original, coherent vision of its social milieu and forges a

3

distinctive style of short fiction. Certainly, Joyce's conception of short fiction is much different from Hughes's, and *Dubliners* exerted more influence on short fiction worldwide; but as a powerful first collection of stories, *The Ways of White Folks* invites comparison to Joyce's important book.

Like other landmark collections, *The Ways of White Folks* draws its power from several sources. For instance, it exhibits a wide range of narrative techniques—deliberately unsentimental, third-person narration, epistolary form, peripheral and "framed" narration, and a variety of interior monologues. In the hands of a lesser writer, such range often appears, at best, self-conscious, at worst, self-indulgent. In Hughes's case, however, the range is handled with such sureness—and form often seems so appropriate to subject—that the effect is one of mastery, not gratuitous display. David Nifong, in discussing Hughes's narrative technique in the collection, praises the "exceptional assortment of narrative perspectives which do not appear as embellishment but prove to be integral parts of an aesthetic whole."[1]

Beyond their technical range, the emotional depth of the stories is also extraordinary. The scope of subjects, characters, and situations explored, the social and political relevance of literary vision, and the unmistakable maturity of that vision also account for the force Hughes's first collection projects.

The Place of *The Ways of White Folks* within Hughes's Career

A few additional biographical circumstances appear to have influenced the power and sureness of Hughes's first collection of short fiction; they warrant brief mention before we discuss *The Ways of White Folks* in detail, because they show the relationship of that book to Hughes's whole career.

Hughes had dabbled in short fiction, writing some stories in high school and then, in his midtwenties, writing a series of three narratives that sprang from his sea travels. To some extent these stories are travel sketches, vividly recapturing the ambience of West Africa, providing glimpses of sailors' lives. James Emanuel has rightly called "Bodies In The Moonlight," which is a brief coming-of-age story, the most accomplished of the three and characterizes it as "the presentation of the theme of initiation into the practical world."[2] Emanuel also notes that Hughes himself called the stories "commercial," written quickly in the summer of 1927 for *The Messenger*, the Harlem publication which Wallace Thurman and George Schuyler edited and in which the three stories appeared (Emanuel, 176). Hughes never included the stories in his short-fiction collections.

The Ways of White Folks, therefore, is clearly a book of Hughes's midcareer. It was published eight years after his first book, a collection of poetry called *The Weary Blues* (1926) that dramatically launched his publishing career.

Hughes was 32 in 1934. He had survived many familial, emotional, and financial crises and had traveled as extensively as any writer of his generation, including Hemingway. He had already visited, often lived in, and in many cases written about Mexico, Europe, Africa, Haiti, Russia, Japan, and the American North, Midwest, South, and West. The Harlem Renaissance had come and gone, leaving Hughes with deep ambivalence about such an artistic movement, the nature of white artistic patronage, the fate of African Americans in American society, and the connections between art, politics, sexuality, and society.

To some extent, then, *The Ways of White Folks* closes an early phase of Hughes's life and literary career and opens a new, more sober one. By the time he published his first collection of stories, Hughes had certainly seen the world, and had already established himself as an important new American voice. Politically, he was entering his most radical phase. He studied class conflict and other Marxist ideas and ruminated on the inequities of American society—inequities the Great Depression had only deepened.

The Ways of White Folks, Modernism, and "Signifying"

Both in the context of Hughes's career and American literature in general, *The Ways of White Folks* represents a convergence of several influences and traditions. At first glance, the collection's unyielding use of irony seems to link it with the modernism of Eliot and Pound, at least in this sense: like these poets and other modernists, Hughes is dissociated from the mainstream of his culture; the *causes* of his dissociation may differ significantly, but the degree does not. Further, the book's edge of social criticism associates Hughes with writers of the modern period, such as Sinclair Lewis and John Dos Passos, whose work also revealed acute social conscience.

However, the work of D. H. Lawrence is the most specific link between Hughes's writing and modernism. The unabashed directness of social criticism in *The Ways of White Folks* shows Lawrence's influence—in fact, Hughes's reading of him led directly to a sustained period of writing short stories.

As biographer Arnold Rampersad has explained, Hughes wrote several of the stories later collected in *The Ways of White Folks* quite suddenly in 1931 when he was in the Soviet Union, ostensibly to work on an ill-fated film project called "Black and White."[3] The visit to the Soviet Union was also an outgrowth of Hughes's leftist politics; he had been a member of the John Reed Club since 1930 and had increasingly perceived the plight of African Americans in economic, "class," and Marxist terms.

While Hughes was in Moscow, a friend encouraged him to read Lawrence's *The Lovely Lady*, a collection of stories. As Rampersad makes clear, Hughes was deeply affected by the stories, specifically by their boldness, directness, and sharp edge of social critique. Lawrence's stories seemed to reveal possibilities for short fiction Hughes had not seen before.

Encountering Lawrence's short fiction impelled Hughes to write "Slave on the Block," "Cora Unashamed," and "Poor Little Black Fellow." In Rampersad's words, Hughes "stressed the volatile mixture of race, class, and sexuality behind not only his troubles with Mrs. Mason [a white patron], but also the rituals of liberal race relations in the United States" (Rampersad, I:269). Other stories in the collection were written after Hughes returned from the Soviet Union, but these too sprang from a brief, furious period of creativity.

In a sense, then, the general growth of Hughes's political awareness fused with the specific example of Lawrence's fiction to create a literary "chemical reaction;" this produced not only many of the stories in Hughes's first book of short fiction, but with them the bold realization that stories might be situated in and/or reflect an idea of social conscience in a particular moment in history.

In other ways, the collection reveals characteristics that spring from a distinctly African-American literary tradition not linked to modernism. That is, while the determined use of irony may connect Hughes with the modernists, it also inevitably results from the predicament of African Americans in the United States—where the difference between perceptions of "white folks" and the reality experienced by African Americans was so great that an ironic vision was less a matter of aesthetic choice than one of everyday fact.

In addition to seeing Hughes's use of irony in a modernist context and in connection with the social predicament of African Americans, one may also see it in a third way: as part of a longstanding African tradition of ironic discourse.

In his ground-breaking book, *The Signifying Monkey*, Henry Louis Gates, Jr. traces the development of a trickster figure in African folk and oral traditions—"the signifying monkey." Gates, showing how the trickster figure informs a range of vernacular traditions that make use of verbal improvisation, parody, and irony, also applies the theory to modern African-American literature.

Gates points to Hughes's long poem "Ask Your Mama" as a "superb example" of "the dozens"—an elaborate African-American conversational mode related to the blues and other vernacular traditions, and involving one-upsmanship, elaborate wordplay, and mock-adversarial rhetoric.[4] Gates's analysis clarifies the extent to which Hughes was immersed in vernacular culture.

In addition to "Ask Your Mama," one other obvious example of such "trickster" characteristics in Hughes's writing is the character Simple, the subject of a subsequent chapter in this book. But even such characters as Berry and the narrator of "A Good Job Gone" (both in *The Ways of White Folks*) display some of the apparently simpleminded but actually sophisticated qualities associated with the trickster. Moreover, the fiercely ironic critique of white society that runs throughout the collection exemplifies the kind of outsider status common to the vernacular tradition Gates examines—the trickster as an inveterate outsider.

While Hughes's connection to modernism, via D. H. Lawrence, is crucial, the way in which stories in *The Way of White Folks* draw on African, oral, and folk traditions, as opposed to European, written, and "literary" ones, is equally crucial. As Gates and others have shown, the obvious influence of the blues on Hughes's literary ideas is but one example of this other tradition. This influence, more obvious in the rhythms and diction of his poetry, still appears in the short fiction—Hughes has a sophisticated ear for levels of diction and elements of dialect, a flair for the performance element in many of the monologues, and affinity for an ironic, deceptively sophisticated "blues" worldview. As Houston Baker has observed, "Hughes may be more comprehensible within the framework of Afro-American verbal and musical performance than within the borrowed framework for the description of written inscriptions of cultural metaphor."[5]

Because the river of Langston Hughes's art and politics is the product of many European, American, and African-American tributaries, Hughes's short stories incorporate great linguistic and epistemological variety—in simpler terms, many voices, many points of view, many vocabularies, many concepts of story.

Individual Stories in *The Ways of White Folks*

The Ways of White Folks collects 14 stories, most of which had been published previously, between 1931 and 1934, in periodicals as diverse as *Esquire* and *The Brooklyn Daily Eagle.* The stories present a variety of conflicts between white and black Americans; they feature numerous rural, suburban, and urban settings in several American regions as well as other countries; and they are contemporary, not historical, meaning they take place in the 1920s and 1930s.

"Cora Unashamed," the first story, effectively sets a tone for the collection. It not only suggests Hughes's interest in the Lawrence-inspired social criticism, but also makes use of verbal and situational ironies. The opening sentences of the story reveal the directness of Hughes's style of short fiction, as well as the psychic distance between Hughes and the communities he will explore: "Melton was one of those in-between little places, not large enough to be a town, nor small enough to be a village—that is, a village in the rural, charming sense of the word. Melton had no charm about it."[6]

The bluntness of the narrative voice here simulates the voice in D. H. Lawrence's fiction and suggests the Jamesian distinction between showing and telling did not always hold sway with Hughes. In these first sentences, Hughes is not as interested in creating a mental picture of a place or effacing the narrator as he is in making a sociological judgment. Indeed, in choosing this direct, politically charged style—which is sometimes deliberately plain, unliterary, even rough—Hughes stakes out a stylistic territory that is removed from the highly polished, often lyrical style of James Joyce, Katherine Mansfield, and other writers who defined a particular class of modern short fiction.

By staking out this new stylistic territory, Hughes almost guaranteed that he would be critically dismissed or misread in some circles, a circumstance Berndt Ostendorf has summarized well. Ostendorf's comment, focusing on poetry, still applies to stories like "Cora Unashamed": "[Hughes] began the necessary reconciliation of formal black poets to their folk roots and grass roots audience. Due to the limitations dictated to poets by current taste and decorum, he could not go to the depth of folk truth and honesty, but he went far enough to be called at different times and by different people subversive, prurient, shallow, simplistic, racist, terms which might well apply to oral folk culture when viewed from a literate, formal perspective. Hughes wanted to be as honest as the blues."[7]

The directness of "Cora Unashamed" and other stories in *The Ways of White Folks*, then, springs from a conscious aesthetic choice, not from an inability to master the more lyrical, less overtly political, more stylized short-story form, as defined by James, Chekhov, Joyce, Hemingway, Mansfield, among others. In turn, the aesthetic choice springs in part from the example of the blues and other kinds of folk art, and from a sense that the predicament of African Americans demanded a plainer, perhaps more combative idea of literature's function. Viewed in this context, the appeal D. H. Lawrence held for Hughes seems even more understandable.

Shifting from the general issue of aesthetic choice to a detailed analysis of the protagonist, Cora Jenkins, and the plot of this first story will help define Hughes's notion of "white folks" and their "ways," and thereby build a foundation for analyzing subsequent stories in the collection.

Cora is the long-suffering, poorly paid servant of a middle-class Melton family, the Studevants. Her own family constitutes "the only Negroes in Melton—Thank God!", as the narrator tells us. Her alcoholic father collects junk for a living; her seven brothers and sisters have all left town before the main action of the story takes place. Cora's only "love affair"—a single tryst with a white I.W.W. laborer who smells like the stables in which he works—results in pregnancy. Most of her sisters encounter the same fate. Her lover abandons her, and the child dies of whooping cough.

Somehow Cora endures this hardship and shame; to some extent she is like a humble Dickens heroine, although Hughes avoids framing her character with Dickensian sentimentality. As the years go by—Cora is 40 during the story's main action—she becomes a surrogate mother to the Studevants' youngest daughter, Jessie.

When Jessie later becomes pregnant out of wedlock, Cora offers her emotional support. She tries to intervene on Jessie's behalf with the parents, who will accept none of Cora's advice, practicality, or good will. They spirit Jessie off to Kansas City for an abortion; Jessie returns and dies soon after of complications.

At Jessie's funeral, Cora is no longer able to bear the hypocrisy and denial of the Studevants. In an address to the dead Jessie, she blurts out the truth about Jessie's pregnancy, abortion, and death. She says, "They killed you, honey. They killed you and your child."

To some degree, "Cora Unashamed" serves as a touchstone story for the collection. It shows that the "ways of white folks" are those actions, gestures, choices, and values lying behind what Hughes perceives to be the pretense of "white folks" and the veneer of middle-class white society.

In a sense, Cora's role in the opening story parallels the artistic role Hughes has chosen for himself in writing these stories. As a social critic with a blunt fictional voice and an ironic stance toward his subject, Hughes will unmask "the ways of white folks," just as Cora unmasks the ways of the Studevents in the denouement of "Cora Unashamed."

Cora's unforgivable breach of propriety is twofold: she deals with Jessie's pregnancy directly and compassionately, and she tells the truth at Jessie's funeral. Through Cora's impropriety, Hughes's story implicitly asks, What kind of community—what kind of society—is it that cannot permit such directness, compassion, and unadorned truth?

If "Cora Unashamed" gives readers a clear idea of what Hughes means by "the ways of white folks," the second story, "Slave on the Block," suggests the imaginative breadth with which Hughes will continue to examine these ways. This story takes readers to Harlem and shows them an upper-middle-class white couple—the Carraways—whose racism initially manifests itself, not in direct mistreatment, but in polite condescension: "They were people who went in for Negroes—Michael and Anne—the Carraways. But not in the social-service, philanthropic sort of way, no. They saw no use in helping a race that was already too charming and naive and lovely for words (*Ways*, 19)."

As in "Cora Unashamed," the voice of the narrator is immediately ironic, even sarcastic. Its message is that the Carraways objectify African Americans, seeing them only as art objects (the title of the story refers to a portrait Anne Carraway is painting)—"samples" of a culture they can perceive only in caricature, childlike entertainers, or objects of unexamined psychosexual fantasies.

As one might expect, the plot peels away the veneer of politeness covering the Carraways' real values; in the end the couple is revealed to be as virulently racist as the Studevants of midwest Melton in "Cora Unashamed." One effect of "Slave on the Block," therefore, is to suggest that racist, self-deluding "ways of white folks" cut across boundaries of region and class, even if they do manifest themselves in relationships that are superficially different, in different regions and social situations.

More basically, perhaps, the contrast between the first two stories shows an awareness of American region and class attributable, in part, not only to Hughes's early rootlessness and insatiable need to travel in his twenties, but also to his interest in Marxist thought. In any event, the first two stories reveal an informed, well-traveled, even cosmopolitan vision behind the deceptively simple, accessible prose style.

The stories "Home" and "Passing" address, respectively, an act of violence and a paradox of racial identity that are both central to the African-American experience: the horror of lynching and the dilemma of "mulattos" who can, if they choose, "pass" as whites.

In "Home," a young but ailing jazz musician returns from Europe to his hometown and is beaten and lynched for tipping his hat to a white woman—his former music teacher, who had, on the same day, invited him to play music in her class. Whereas in "Slave On the Block," the psychosexual tension is indirect, in "Home" it is explicit: a black man who tips his hat to a white woman violates a taboo.

In "Passing," a young black man writes a letter to his mother, telling her why he had to ignore her on the street and explaining what the accursed gift of "passing" means in his life.

These two stories enlarge the scope of the collection in at least two important ways. Most obviously, by concerning themselves with lynching and passing, they embrace topics that are symbolically resonant but were also matters of everyday African-American reality in Hughes's time. Lynching is an apotheosis of racist hatred; passing is an apotheosis of the African-American crisis of identity in a hostile culture.

In addition to broadening the symbolic reach of the collection, these two stories demonstrate Hughes's stylistic range. In "Cora Unashamed" and "Slave on the Block," Hughes relies on an ironic, third-person narrator who seems distant from the subject but hardly invisible to the reader. In "Home," he mixes stream-of-consciousness techniques with the third-person point of view, and in "Passing," he uses a first-person letter form.

"Passing" also adds something new to the collection by portraying the psychic consequences of "the ways of white folks." Obviously, we see the effects of racism on black characters in the first three stories of the volume, but these effects are dramatized overtly: Cora finally explodes at Jessie's funeral, for example, and Roy Williams is lynched. In "Passing," however, we get a glimpse of the psychic cost of racism before it reaches a crisis point.

To be sure, the narrator has already had to choose to ignore his mother in public, a choice that amounts to a crisis. But because his relationship with whites has not erupted into violence or some other irrevocable rift, we glimpse the psychic dilemma of one who has found the means, and has chosen to use them, of being accepted into "the ways of white folks." In one sense, "Passing" is a simpler, less ambitious story than its predecessors, but it nonetheless adds an important dimension to the collection.

Like "Slave on the Block," "A Good Job Gone" and "Rejuvenation through Joy" are stories of New York City. The former features a peripheral narrator who witnesses, reports, and suffers the consequences of a disintegrating relationship between his boss—a white businessman whose wife is disabled—and his boss's black mistress. While "A Good Job Gone" ends as bleakly as "Cora Unashamed" and "Home"—the boss goes insane and dies—its luckless, unsophisticated, but undaunted narrator prefigures Simple, Hughes's magnificent comic creation who would appear in the 1940s. The story, which contains some of the "signifying monkey" traits discussed earlier in this chapter, also has a narrator with a bit of the naive Huckleberry Finn about him. While he faithfully reports a relationship that reflects complex sexual, racial, and ethnic issues, his central concern is losing a cushy job. At some level, he knows his boss's affair exemplifies unequal power relationships capitalizing on race, gender, and social class. But he is most conscious of his own powerlessness and need to survive.

Spanning 30 pages, "Rejuvenation through Joy" is the longest story in the collection. In it Hughes transforms the irony of the first several stories into full-blown satire. The story traces the career of Eugene Lesch, a former circus performer. With his manager Sol, Lesch has formed the Colony of Joy, a 1930s version of a New Age cult; it "rejuvenates" well-heeled white patrons through the natural "joys" of "primitive Negro culture, such as dancing.

To a degree, "Rejuvenation through Joy" is similar to "Slave On The Block" because it is concerned with how African Americans are objectified, patronized, labeled "primitive," and then used as means through which whites achieve pleasure. But here the broad comedy and satire blur lines between black and white, until everyone involved in Lesch's scam comes off as foolish at best, vicious at worst. One might say the story shows Hughes at his most Swiftian, when all of humanity seems barely worth the effort.

Nevertheless, one bedrock idea remains: the ways of white folks include ways of using blacks in shameless scams, chiefly through exploiting racial stereotypes. In this regard, "Rejuvenation through Joy" is one expression of the ambivalence with which Hughes viewed the Harlem Renaissance—although it was a flowering of African-American art and thought in America's most important cultural metropolis, it was also another instance of exploitation. Harlem, African-American art (or "Negro" art, as it was called in Hughes's era), and what Zora Neale Hurston had labeled the "niggerati," all became "experiences" for the self-centered, self-serving white tourists who visited Harlem. From this perspective, the Harlem Renaissance was anything but an age of enlightenment. It became, instead, as satirized by "Rejuvenation through Joy," a more complicated phase of exploitation.

"Red-Headed Baby" may be the least formally successful story in the collection. Because the speaker addresses a specific listener within the frame of the story, it is a dramatic, not an interior, monologue. The point of view draws attention to itself, however, mainly because Hughes seems uncomfortable with the diction. Sometimes we sense that Hughes himself wanted to gravitate toward a more conventional third-person narration in which dialogue is simply reported.

Like "Good Job Gone," "Red-Headed Baby" addresses sexual and romantic relationships between white men and black women; in this case, a drunken sailor living on the Florida coast visits a young woman who has given birth to their child. Of all Hughes's narrators in *The Ways of White Folks*, the sailor is the most sordid and disintegrated, the setting the most squalid. Even if the narrative vehicle seems unsatisfactory or undeveloped, the story no doubt let Hughes make use of his own experience on steamers and in backwater ports, and let him address the exploitation of young, impoverished black women.

In a social and regional context, "Poor Little Black Fellow" is "Red-Headed Baby's" opposite. Set in aristocratic New England, the story involves a wealthy couple that raises the orphaned black child of former servants; the father has been killed in the Great War, and the mother has died of pneumonia. The decision to raise the orphan seems an act of great generosity, but as in "Slave on the Block," the goodwill is a veneer. A trip to Paris when the young man is of college age finally strips away all pretense, exposes the deep racism of the couple, and results in the young man's decision to stay in Paris. While readers of the collection will have come to expect the situational irony of this story, the role of Paris as safe haven for African Americans, hinted at in "Home," is explored here fully for the first time. In this sense the story demonstrates one irony encountered by African-American soldiers in the Great War: the "foreign" city of Paris treated them with greater respect than their "home" cities did—an irony that Richard Wright and James Baldwin also explored in their essays and novels.

Moreover—beneath the overt situational irony—"Poor Little Black Fellow" is also a poignant coming-of-age story: Paris is the site of the young man's healthy initiation; it allows him to move on.

Of the remaining stories in the collection, "The Blues I'm Playing," "Berry," "Mother and Child," and "Father and Son" particularly warrant discussion because of their complexity and verve, and also because they explore a variety of relationships based on power. "The Blues I'm Playing" examines the intricate relationship between a wealthy white patron, a woman, and a young African-American woman who plays the piano. That parallels exist between this story and Hughes's own tumultuous relationship with the wealthy New York patron Charlotte (Mrs. Rufus Osgood) Mason is obvious; however, the story is not simply a veiled piece of autobiography.

As the relationship between Oceola Jones (the pianist) and Dora Ellsworth (the patron) develops, it becomes clear Mrs. Ellsworth is not interested just in supporting Oceola and her art, but in reshaping both. Specifically, Mrs. Ellsworth projects her own fastidiousness and fear of men onto Oceola, warning her that Oceola's lover will "take the music out of you" (*Ways*, 119). Indeed, a sexual undercurrent runs throughout the relationship between Oceola and her patron. Further, Mrs. Ellsworth wants Oceola to play only classical music and not work with the variations on spirituals and the blues that Oceola has explored.

To some extent, the story explores themes of cultural exploitation similar to those in "Slave on the Block," but the relationship between Oceola and Mrs. Ellsworth is far more complex than that between the Carraways and the African Americans they attempt to "help." For one thing, Mrs. Ellsworth is a genuine patron of the arts, and she does support Oceola substantially for many years. Nonetheless, the resolution of the story makes clear that while a relationship of patronage may take longer to reveal itself as yet another relationship of racism and power, it will inevitably do so. In their last meeting, Oceola cannot resist playing for Mrs. Ellsworth "the soft and lazy syncopation of a Negro blues, a blues that deepened and grew into rollicking jazz (*Ways*, 119)." Mrs. Ellsworth is offended: "Is this what I spent thousands of dollars to teach you?" (*Ways*, 120). The patronage ends.

Clearly, "The Blues I'm Playing" let Hughes work out in fictional terms the difficult relationship he had with his own patron. But the story also let him deconstruct what he took to be a false distinction between "high" and "low" art, and it let him expose what he took to be the prudish pretentiousness of aristocratic patrons. In fact, the story connects prudishness or repressed sexuality with matters of artistic judgement because it suggests Mrs. Ellsworth's rigid artistic categories are a projection of her fear of sensuousness and earthiness, as expressed by Oceola's personal life and her music.

To a degree, "Berry" echoes themes defined in "Cora Unashamed." Like Cora, Milberry, the main character, is the only African American in a white community, in this case a home for crippled children in New Jersey. Like Cora, Milberry is not formally educated but is intuitively moral and just.

The home exploits him economically, and it does so as ruthlessly as the Studevants exploit Cora. But whereas Cora ends up deliberately indicting the Studevants' hypocrisy, Milberry exposes the dishonesty and heartlessness of the home unwittingly by giving the children the emotional nourishment they've been denied. He is fired for doing so, of course.

In addition to reworking economic, racial, and moral issues that "Cora Unashamed" introduced, "Berry" also provides the title and epigraph to the collection, both taken from this key passage. "Besides," Milberry said to himself, 'the ways of white folks, I mean some white folks, is too much for me. I reckon they must be a few good ones, but most of 'em ain't good—leastwise they don't treat me good. And Lawd knows, I ain't never done nothin' to 'em, nothin' a-tall'" (*Ways*, 275).

Of all the stories in the collection, "Mother and Child" most obviously reveals Hughes-the-dramatist, the writer who often wanted to transmit and express everything through dialogue. It is in any case a more successful experiment with narration-through-dialogue than "Red-Headed Baby." The story tells of the birth of a baby, fathered by a black farmer in small Ohio town. The mother is white and married to someone else. The events come to us entirely through the dialogue—the gossip, if you will—of several African-American women as they wait for a meeting of the Salvation Rock Ladies Missionary Society for the Rescue o' the

African Heathen, a name that amounts to a self-contained send up of small-town religion. Through the dialogue, Hughes reveals not only the white community's horrified response to the child's birth but also the narrow-minded, self-righteous response of these church ladies.

Both the guiding tone and the resolution of "Mother and Child" are more comic than tragic; in this way the story anticipates the ethos of Hughes's second collection, *Laughing To Keep From Crying* (1952). Thematically, however, the story is consistent with other stories in *The Ways of White Folks*—"Cora Unashamed," "Slave on the Block," "A Good Job Gone," "Red-Headed Baby," and "The Blues I'm Playing"—insofar as it links the socioeconomic and sexual manifestations of racial conflict in America.

Whether "Father and Son" is Hughes's "best-crafted fiction," as R. Baxter Miller has suggested, is open to debate; nonetheless, the story is indisputably one of Hughes's most ambitious and most tragic narratives.[8] In it the aforementioned socioeconomic and sexual dimensions of American racial conflict reach their fullest expression within the collection, and the gothic elements and enlarged scope of the story are similar to those in Faulkner's short fiction.

"Father and Son" concerns a white plantation owner, Colonel Norwood, and Bert, his mulatto son, who has returned from college. Throughout Bert's life the Colonel has attempted to deny Bert is his son; but the Colonel also recognizes that Bert, particularly in his defiant, willful ways, is more like him than are any of his other children. In the relentless, superbly structured tragedy that follows, the Colonel collapses and dies when confronted with the choice of killing Bert or acknowledging him as his son. Accused of killing the Colonel, Bert is hunted by a mob and ultimately kills himself to deprive the mob of the satisfaction of lynching him. His body is burned and posthumously lynched at a crossroads.

In addition to exploring the many dilemmas of the mulatto, "Father and Son" also successfully represents the consciousness of all the crucial participants—the colonel, his mistress Cora, Bert, the lynch mob. The story exhibits Hughes's use of the third-person, omniscient point of view at its most successful.

"Father and Son" reworks many of the key economic, social, and sexual conflicts that preceding stories in the collection presented, giving them their most terrible, consequential, and mythic formulation. R. Baxter Miller had usefully connected the tragic scope of this story with the infamous Scottsboro case, which had enormous impact on Hughes:

"The narrator of ["Father and Son"] makes clear the disintegration of the communal and holy bond. But the symbolic oppositions between Norwood and Bert run more deeply. To [Hughes] the metaphors of uncleanliness—responses that are intense, moral, and personal as well as mythic—go back to the Scottsboro boys, falsely accused in 1931 of raping two white prostitutes" (Miller, 105).

The rage and sexual hysteria that provokes the lynch mobs and the Colonel's denial of his own son in "Home" and "Father and Son" spring, therefore, from the same source that led to the Scottsboro "witch hunt." False accusations of sexual crimes and the inability to acknowledge one's own sexual history are connected, Hughes suggests, to a projection of sexual frustration onto a scapegoat—an objectified African American.

Summary

The stories in *The Ways of White Folks* took shape at a crucial moment in Hughes's life and writing career. To some extent, the moment was one of self doubt, for his literary fame and the heady whirlwind of the Harlem Renaissance had waned, leaving Hughes ambivalent at best, embittered at worst. Marxist ideas and a general concern with the economic plight of African Americans influenced him greatly and were reinforced by his troubles with a wealthy white patron of the arts, Charlotte Mason.

At this crucial moment, reading D. H. Lawrence's stories seemed to convince Hughes that short fiction was an excellent medium through which to express his frustrations, to represent intertwined conflicts of race, sex, and economics in America, and to take advantage of the many regional and social venues, in America and abroad, where Hughes had seen racial strife take place.

The stories in *The Ways of White Folks* exhibit a Marxist influence in the general sense that Hughes's awareness of economic forces and social stratification informs them, but not in the sense that they propagandize, or promote any kind of Marxist Utopia, Russian or otherwise. Hughes's experience with Marxist ideas and with Lawrence's writing broadened the conceptual scope of his social critique. The experience gave him a greater variety of ways in which to perceive ethnic and racial conflict; it did not overwhelm his art or give it a political monotone.

In any event, *The Ways of White Folks* stands as one of Hughes's most important, unified, and accomplished works. It is a landmark book in his career, in the canon of African-American literature, and in the history of

American short fiction. Its social criticism seems bold and relevant even today; its implicit concept of short fiction as a form of social critique links Hughes with Lawrence and sets his short stories apart from the more self-consciously polished, more lyrical, and less explicitly political short story as defined by James Joyce, Katherine Mansfield, and Ernest Hemingway.

Laughing to Keep from Crying

Overview: Mining a Comic Vein

Laughing To Keep From Crying (Henry Holt, 1952) contains 24 stories, most of which had appeared earlier in such magazines as *The African, American Spectator, Crisis, Esquire, The New Yorker,* and *Story.*

A collection of Jesse B. Simple stories had appeared in 1950 from Simon and Schuster: *Simple Speaks His Mind.* Since the Simple stories represent a separate, distinct development in Hughes's short fiction, however, this chapter refers to *Laughing To Keep From Crying* as the "second" collection, meaning the second gathering of stories not featuring Simple. Further, since Hughes did not fully develop Simple until later in the 1950s, there is a sense in which the collection represents the middle portion of Hughes's progress as a writer of stories.

As the title of the collection suggests, Hughes seems to have decided to let his short fiction mine a vein of comedy. One indelible impression created by *The Ways of White Folks* is of black and white Americans on unavoidable collision courses, in every region and social class of the land. In contrast, most of the stories in *Laughing To Keep From Crying* leave the impression that black Americans will survive the collisions, and that the nature and consequences of the collisions are sometimes unpredictable. In his second collection, Hughes is by no means less unflinching in his documentation of the African-American predicament, but he generally shifts the focus from destructive consequences to embodiments of resiliency.

As in the first collection, irony, often of the situational kind, plays a key role in *Laughing To Keep From Crying.* The irony, however, often gravitates toward comedy rather than satire or tragedy. To some extent, this shift in purpose or temperament reveals a desire to accept and to heal. It would be overgeneralizing to say that Hughes's short fiction journeys from outrage to acceptance in the years between his first and second collections; the transformation was not that simple, complete, or one-dimensional. Nonetheless, a comic spirit makes *Laughing To Keep From Crying* a much different collection of stories.

The greatest similarity between the two collections is narrative technique. As this chapter will reveal, a broader range of form exists in the second book, but overall Hughes is still writing with great directness and simplicity; he is embracing a variety of characters and settings; he is letting social criticism infiltrate and shape his fiction.

The story "Who's Passing For Who?" offers specific clues to the general differences and similarities between the two collections of stories. Suggesting changes in Hughes's outlook on racial conflict, it seems a universe apart from the last story of *The Ways of White Folks*, the mythic, tragic "Father and Son."

In this first story of the collection, three apparently white middle-class tourists visit Harlem to "sample" black culture—a situation that is not so different from those presented in *The Ways of White Folks*, where the idea of sampling or experiencing culture was exposed as another symptom of racism. In "Who's Passing For Who?" one of the characters says, without irony or self-consciousness, "We've never met a Negro writer before."[9]

In the course of the story, the three tourists (Iowans, we learn) and several black artists sit down for drinks in a club. A black patron at another table strikes his female companion during an argument. One of the men defends the woman, whom he thinks is white. During the ensuing verbal argument, he finds out the woman is actually black, and he apologizes for butting in. One of the black artists then asks him why defending the woman became less important when the man found out she was black. The man storms off, leaving his friends from Iowa—a "white" couple—behind. At the end of the story, this couple reveals they are black and have been merely passing as white.

As in the stories of *The Ways of White Folks*, the ironies of the situation are obvious, the plot streamlined, the style direct, colloquial, unadorned. One chief difference, however, is that Hughes allows the essential situational irony to multiply into further ironies until the situation becomes ridiculous. Consequently, the story moves beyond the theme of whites "sampling" black Harlem culture and teases the whole question of skin color until the question unravels comically. At the end of the story, the first-person plural narrator remarks, "Whatever race they [the 'white' couple] were, they had had too much fun at our expense—even if they did pay for the drinks" (*Laughing*, 7).

Does the story imply that questions of skin color are moot, promoting the stale platitude "we're all the same underneath"? No. Despite the shift toward comedy, Hughes still shows an awareness of the deep ethnic differences history, law, and economics have created. He also shows how attitudes toward women are affected by attitudes toward color.

The shift toward comedy, then, is clear, but measured. Hughes is exploring the complications, many of them potentially comic, of "race relations," but he is not playing down the existence of deep social inequities.

The use of "we" as narrator of "Who's Passing For Who?" to some extent contributes to the comic ethos of the story because it admits multiple perspectives on the action of the story. In a sense, this first-person plurality represents the ambivalence with which the story approaches the topic of "passing"—an ambivalence greater than in the story "Passing" from *The Ways of White Folks*, where the first-person epistolary form reinforces a single, isolated perspective.

"Something In Common" may be the most predictable and least satisfying story of the collection. In it, an elderly black man and an elderly white man meet in a Hong Kong bar, spar verbally, nearly come to blows, get kicked out by the British bartender, and then decide to join forces against the bartender. For the moment, nationalism is more powerful than race. The situation seems far more contrived and less believable than that in "Who's Passing For Who?", and the texture of irony far less complicated. Nonetheless, the story reinforces the sense that Hughes is using irony for comic, rather than satiric, purposes.

In part because it follows the thin, predictable story, "Something In Common," "African Morning" is a delightful surprise and one of Hughes's most memorable stories. "African Morning" works with a version of "the tragic mulatto," a recurring character type in Hughes's stories and in much African-American and southern literature symbolizing the consequences and dilemmas of racism.

A young mulatto African boy is sent by his father, a white banker, on an errand to the waterfront of a city. The boy is mistaken for a prostitute's son, teased, beaten, and chased. At the end of the story, the boy confronts the tragedy of being "the color of gold" (*Laughing*, 19). He realizes that, because his mother is dead, his father will find it easy to abandon him. He then dives into a pool, wishes to drown, but bobs up like a cork; bright birds land on a branch overhead, then fly away.

"African Morning" is more visually rich and evocative than many of Hughes's stories; in it a Joycean sense of epiphany provides a strategy for closure not often seen in Hughes's short fiction. This story also depends less on situational ironies for its effect, and more on the pathos of the main character.

The symbolism of "the color of gold" is also striking because at some level both the boy and reader come to realize that in Africa, at that particular historical moment, to be a "gold" mulatto is to be, in some sense, a form of currency. That is, the boy represents literal and figurative commerce between Europe and Africa; he understands his status as mulatto has reduced him to an object in most people's eyes, a kind of human coin.

To a degree, "African Morning" differs from the stories that precede and follow it in the collection because it is more dramatic, even tragic, than comic. The ending of the story, however, suggests the boy's resilience, and the bright birds—which can in one sense be taken as a symbol for an unconcerned, morally neutral universe—also add an image of spontaneous beauty that relieves the dominant, somber tone. Even while working with the figure of the tragic mulatto, Hughes does not close himself off to a certain inspiriting element.

"Saratoga Rain," a highly lyrical, compressed, one-page story, offers surprises not unlike those in "African Morning." Evocative and imagistic, it is almost a prose-poem description of two lovers, both gamblers, who achieve a temporary peace one rainy morning in Saratoga. We find out that although their relationship has been plagued by adultery and other dishonesties, they have entered a redemptive moment. "Saratoga Rain" will remind many readers of several Ernest Hemingway stories—"Hills Like White Elephants" or "Cat In The Rain"—which deal with troubled "modern" couples. The tone and method of closure are more generous, more positive, perhaps more earthy in Hughes's story than in these Hemingway pieces, but both writers provide a highly polished, intense glimpse of a moment in conjoined lives.

"Spanish Blood" is perhaps most notable as a slice-of-Harlem-nightclub-life, and "Heaven To Hell" is a very light, comic monologue spoken by a woman who has been in an automobile accident with her husband. When a woman the narrator supposes to be her husband's mistress visits her, the narrator is consumed with jealousy and narrow-minded piety.

"Sailor Ashore" is a more ambitious story than these other two. Set in Los Angeles, it adds another point to Hughes's immense fictional map, draws successfully on his knowledge of waterfronts and the seagoing life, and uses dialogue and colloquial language adeptly. A sailor and a prostitute—both black—meet and seek temporary solace with one another, but end up only reinforcing their sense of despair and hopelessness. In its own way, "Sailor Ashore," is as poignant in its depiction of two disenfranchised characters, as "African Morning" is in its depiction of a tragic mulatto.

Linked with Sailor Ashore" (set in Los Angeles), "Slice Him Down" and "Tain't So," set, respectively, in Reno and Hollywood, begin to suggest what the American West meant to Hughes—less a frontier or otherwise physical landscape, more an unpredictable, embryonic social province of America. Hughes does not, to be sure, idealize the West, but he does suggest how it is a unique North American region.

"Slice Him Down" takes place in a Reno bar and features two older African-American drinking buddies whose bragging escalates into a knife fight in which layers of clothing insure no one gets seriously injured. "Tain't So" details the visit of a "proper" Southern white woman to a black faith healer and fortune-teller in Hollywood. The essential situations keep the stories well within the comic boundaries of the collection.

Beyond North and South, however, the stories also hint at a third regional dimension to the predicament of race in America. *The Ways of White Folks* often presented racial conflict as it emerged in brutal dichotomies: master/servant; patron/artist; rich/poor; and most especially, North/South.

In these stories set in the American West, racial strife and its consequences haven't disappeared: Reno has its "black" or "Negro" side of town; Los Angeles is not more economically hopeful for blacks than Chicago or New York. Nonetheless, the unrelenting nature of racism is somewhat relieved, and the relief seems to spring from the relatively unhardened youth of the West. The "black" side of Reno isn't as oppressed or victimized as Harlem; the scuffle depicted in "Slice Him Down," between two black men, ends comically, very much a family affair. The African-American faith healer is comfortably esconced in flaky Hollywood, making her way.

Perhaps more importantly, a sense of blurred—if not erased—racial lines, and a region in flux emerges in these stories. Each story refers in its own way to racism, but the racism has often been defanged, most obviously in "Tain't So." And in all three stories, the social boundaries are less fixed. For instance, when Miss Lucy, the "proper" white Southern woman in "Tain't So," remarks, "I'll never in the world get used to the North. Now here's a great—my friend says great faith-healer, treating darkies!" (*Laughing*, 80), we know she is really put off by a particularly western variety of northernness. She realizes as much herself when she discovers the faith healer is black, and the faith healer heals her psyche simply by disagreeing with her. Certainly, Miss Lucy's racism isn't "harmless"; no racism is, as Hughes shows repeatedly in his fiction. But Miss Lucy is harmless.

Few readers would likely call "One Friday Morning" or "Professor" the most compelling or most comic stories of *Laughing To Keep From Crying*; in fact, both seem plodding and uninspired in contrast to "African Morning," "Saratoga Rain," and "On The Road." Taken together, however, the two stories are of particular note because they concern two African Americans who choose to beat the racist system by changing it from within. "On Friday Morning" presents a young African-American woman who wins an art award, only to have it taken away when the judging committee discovers her skin color. Her response? At the high school awards ceremony, she stands up, recites the Pledge of Allegiance with everyone else, and says to herself: "That is the land we must make" (*Laughing*, 95).

The story is surprisingly unironic, unembittered, even sentimental for Hughes, but it serves to prepare the way for "Professor." It also suggests Hughes was considering—not endorsing, but considering—methods, which did not come naturally to him, of coping with racism.

In the second of these "paired" stories, a professor from a black college visits a philanthropic white family, the Chandlers, at none other than the Booker T. Washington Hotel, in itself a symbol for working within the system.

The professor, Dr. Brown, tells the Chandlers what they want to hear and allows them to condescend to him because he knows he can get money for the impoverished college: "And the things Dr. Brown's little college needed were small enough in the eyes of the Chandlers. The sane and conservative way in which Dr. Brown presented his case delighted the philanthropic heart of the Chandlers. And Mr. Chandler and Dr. Bulwick both felt that instead of building a junior college for Negroes in their own town they could rightfully advise local colored students to go down South to that fine little campus where they had a professor of their own race like Dr. Brown" (*Laughing*, 105). The ironic tone here lets us know Hughes certainly has not lost his skepticism, even cynicism, about "the ways of white (philanthropic) folks." But as in

"One Friday Morning," an ambivalence toward working within the system emerges.

Hughes clearly is not enthusiastically endorsing the responses of the girl cheated out of her prize nor those of the professor who "grins and bears" condescension. But neither is he indicting or heaping scorn on them.

Instead, the stories to some extent document a social or economic form of passing that involves a figurative blending in: a willingness to take the Pledge of Allegiance at face value and push the society toward an ideal it has never tried to achieve, and to use philanthropy motivated by racism for a greater good, a willingness to "go along to get along."

Although Hughes himself briefly had a white patron, and although he worked with all manner of mainstream editors and publishers, his style was not to conform as completely or with as much docility as these two characters. Nonetheless, by admitting such conformist characters into his fictional world without satirizing them, Hughes showed a measure of disinterestedness, at least, and perhaps even generosity toward African Americans who chose to cope in ways that did not personally suit him.

In the four stories, "Pushcart Man," "Why, You Reckon?" "Name in the Papers," and "Rouge High," the plots are minimal, and the inclination is to fashion sketches of street life in New York City, or at least of street characters that embodied such life as Hughes viewed it.

"Pushcart Man," for instance, is a kind of prose-poem filled with street speech; it creates a miniature folk opera of numerous arguments, conversations, sales pitches, and monologues on a Harlem street. While the pushcart man constitutes a kind of unifying musical theme, there is no main character, action, or pointed message to the story. Sound, its exuberant flow, is the sense of the piece.

In "Why, You Reckon?" a young upper-middle-class white man is mugged and responds enthusiastically; to the befuddlement of his muggers, he thinks of the event as a way to experience black culture. Here the familiar notion of "sampling culture" returns at its most absurd, perhaps, and mugging is presented in its most pleasant light—pleasant enough to appear in *The New Yorker*.

"Name In The Papers" is a monologue spoken by a hospitalized man who has just been shot several times by a husband who discovered his wife and the speaker in compromising circumstances. The speaker is much less concerned with his ventilated body than with the possibility of having his name appear in the newspaper.

"Rouge High" depicts two prostitutes in a bar; a pimp walks in, strikes one of the women, takes money from her, and leaves. For both the women and the bartender the incident seems de rigueur. The woman then produces a money-choked wallet lifted from a customer, making it clear the pimp only thought he was getting his due. The other woman tells her that her eye is swelling from the beating and suggests she "rouge high"—move the rouge up from cheekbone to eye.

The theme of undaunted resilience, the mixture of naive and worldly-wise humor, the attention to dialect and speech patterns, and the minimalist "sketch" form in these four stories all bear strong resemblance to the Jesse B. Simple stories Hughes had begun to write for *The Chicago Defender* and which he had already collected in one book.[10]

As we have seen, one obvious difference between Hughes's first and second collections is that *Laughing To Keep From Crying* shows a shift in purpose, tone, and narrative mode, toward the comic. This shift did not mean that Hughes turned away completely from depicting the devastating consequences of racism; the stories "African Morning" and "Sailor Ashore," already discussed, demonstrate as much. The stories "Powder-White Faces" and "On The Way Home" also go against the dominant comic grain of the collection. In fact, of all the stories in *Laughing To Keep From Crying*, these two concern themselves most deeply with the desperation racism creates.

In "Powder-White Faces," Hughes creates a more deadly version of the illicit romantic situation that underlies comic stories such as "A Good Job Gone" or "Name in the Papers." A Chinese-American youth who has changed his name and jumped aboard a tramp steamer relates in flashback how he murdered a white woman with whom he was involved. The motive, purely and simple, is rage at being belittled, at being called "China boy."

The story is remarkable, in part, for the way in which it addresses racist-inspired rage so directly and places racism in a context that isn't African-American. Further, it deals with a kind of ferocity that is out of key with the dominant tone of the collection.

"On The Way Home" is in no sense as violent as "Powder-White Faces," but it locates itself in a similar desperation. It depicts an alcoholic African-American man whose mother is dying. Unable to bring himself to visit her, he sinks further into alcohol as the story proceeds. Like "Powder-White Faces," the story makes the desperate person's point of view sympathetic, even though it may not be completely acceptable or exemplary; like most of the stories in *Laughing To Keep From Crying*, it describes the cost of a difficult life made even more difficult by a racist society.

The stories "Mysterious Madame Shanghai," "Little Old Spy," and "Baths" do not share common themes, settings, or narrative techniques, but in one sense they belong together because they seem to spring from Hughes's restless, itinerant life. All three are reportorial in nature, though the narrative structures and points of view differ; of all the stories in the collection, these seem to be the ones least transformed by fictional reshaping.

Hughes sets "Mysterious Madame Shanghai" in a New York boarding house, a locale frequently used in Hughes's fiction, second only to bars. The story details the lengthy, strange, exotic relationship between a former circus performer, Madam Shanghai, and her husband. Racial or ethnic conflict has little bearing on the story; Hughes seems chiefly to be retrieving from his travels an offbeat tale of cruel love.

Much the same can be said for "Baths," a story of ill-fated love set in Mexico and of "Little Old Spy," which is about the menacing but, in this story at least, ultimately harmless machinations of the reactionary government in Cuba.

All three tales seem deliberately underdramatized: all three blend in with the epistemological sense of ironic acceptance that surrounds the collection; all three bear the mark of Hughes-the-reporter, Hughes-the-documenter; all three link Hughes's fiction stylistically with his two autobiographies, *I Wonder As I Wander* and *The Big Sea*.[11]

In "The Trouble With Angels," "On the Road," and "Big Meeting," Hughes casts a comic, almost satiric, eye toward matters of religion. Certainly, these stories do not approach the broad, lacerating satire of "Rejuvenation Through Joy (*The Ways of White Folks*), but they nonetheless collectively demonstrate Hughes's cynicism on the subject.

"The Trouble With Angels" takes us behind the scenes of a touring gospel musical drama with an African-American cast. The popular production gets booked in Washington, D.C.—where "legitimate playhouses have no accom[m]odations for 'colored people.' Incredible as it may seem, until Ingrid Bergman made her stand, Washington was worse than the Deep South in that respect" (*Laughing*, 174).

Hughes gets a lot of funny, biting mileage out of the hypocritical contrast between the spiritual piety of white audiences and the racism of unwritten public entertainment laws. He also reserves a good deal of cynical wit for the actor playing God— "this colored God who had been such a hit on Broadway" (*Laughing*, 175)—who refuses to join the cast in a strike. This God, Hughes lets us know, is quite human and does not endorse the idea of solidarity as a method of combating racism.

"Big Meeting," by comparison, is relatively free of such implied social criticism. The chief impetus of this story seems to be Hughes's wish to document, even celebrate, that genre of religious convocation known as "the tent meeting" or "camp meeting." At one point, the black narrator remarks on white people who sit in their cars at the periphery of the gathering: "The white people were silent again in their car, listening to the singing. In the dark I couldn't see their faces to tell if they were still amused or not. But that was mostly what they wanted out of Negroes— work and fun—without paying for it, I thought, work and fun" (*Laughing*, 198). This critical assessment of whites—a throwback to *The Ways of White Folks*—is the exception to the predominant tone of "Big Meeting," which is celebratory. Just as "Pushcart Man" captures the "music" of the streets, "Big Meeting" captures the literal and figurative music of a tent meeting.

Despite his cynicism toward spirituality, particularly of the pious kind, and despite his Marxist leanings and his social-critic's perspective, Hughes clearly saw the healing, unifying force the tent meetings provided to working-poor African Americans in the South. "Big Meeting" is at once the most meticulous and generous depiction of such a meeting one is likely to find in American short fiction. It by no means represents an abrupt turn toward religion as a solution to social, economic, or racial ills, but does represent Hughes's acknowledgment of religious ritual as a legitimate source of support for the beleaguered. Whereas the comedy of "Trouble With Angels" edges toward satire, the comedy of "Big Meeting" is full of acceptance, gravitating toward encomium.

It is no wonder that "On The Road" is the most anthologized story from the collection, and—outside of the Jesse B. Simple stories taken as a whole—the best-known Hughes story. A superb short narrative, it shows just how successful Hughes could be in a short-story form which is in sharp contrast to the dominant modernist mode emphasizing image, style, and lyricism over plot.

"On The Road" is a parable that makes almost perfect use of techniques and tendencies found in Hughes's first two collections: the simple, direct style, the thirst for social criticism, the balance between satire and comedy, the basic, easily recognizable plot line, and the ability to create "everyman" characters.

The story depicts Sargeant, a down-and-out African-American drifter who finds himself nearly freezing to death in a snowy northern city. Sargeant tries to hammer his way into a white church to find a warm place to sleep. He sees—and talks with—Christ, in what turns out to be an hallucination.

Sargeant believes he has knocked on the church door so hard that the church has fallen down. Christ thanks him for the liberation: "You had to pull the church down to get me off the cross" (*Laughing*, 187).

Christ turns out to be as bluesy, forlorn, and folksy as Sargeant. He (Christ) is as disappointed in the climatological, social, and spiritual failings of the northern city as Sargeant is, wants to go to Kansas City. After the vision, Sargeant is rudely awakened—in jail.

"On the Road" is a nearly perfectly-wrought, understated modern parable, satisfying on several levels,—at once simple, rich, pointed, and funny. One of its "morals," of course, is a kind of implied question: When will "Christ" (Christian values) come down off the cross and out of the church to do some good in society?

Summary

Laughing To Keep From Crying represents a shift—in tone, outlook, and choice of subject—from the harshly ironic social criticism of *The Ways of White Folks* to a comic but weary, blues-influenced outlook of acceptance.

In matters of narrative technique, however, the differences between the two books are far less extreme. In his second collection, Hughes still relies on simple narrative forms—the tale, the sketch, the parable, and deliberately undramatic reportage. He also remains interested in allowing colloquial language, the blues, gospel music, and the sound and sense of "street speech" to inform the language of his short fiction.

Moreover, the "cosmopolitan Hughes" remains constant in both volumes. Behind his preference for simplicity and directness in narrative form, open-minded, well-traveled geographic, political, and cultural visions remain constant. Indeed, one of the most profound curiosities of Hughes's short fiction is that while his narrative choices are often similar to those of self-proclaimed regionalists and local colorists, his concept of society and culture is multinational and eclectic.

Working with a variety of seemingly naive but actually very knowing characters, Hughes shows in his second collection the degree to which the "consciousness" of Jesse B. Simple—which had been taking shape since 1942 in *The Chicago Defender* columns—haunted him and shaped his writing.

Many critics have noted the irony of *Laughing To Keep From Crying* appearing in the same year as Ralph Ellison's *Invisible Man* (1952). Within the tradition of African-American writing, it was as if a torch of literary mastery were being passed from the older writer to the younger, and from simpler narrative forms to more complex, even mythic ones. While Hughes's collection was overshadowed by Ellison's monumental book, however, it is worth noting that the two writers shared an acute interest in issues of class and economics and that both relied heavily on irony as a method of rendering their fiction. Such commonalities make the books seem more like complementary expressions of a similar vision than competing works from writers of different generations. In any case, the older writer Hughes was yet to realize fully his most enduring short fiction character, one of the most indelible characters in American literature: Jesse B. Simple.

The Jesse B. Simple Stories and *Something in Common*

Introduction

This chapter examines Langston Hughes's single most important and enduring achievement in short fiction: the creation and development of Jesse B. Simple—part buffoon, sage, folk hero, comedian, witness, and trickster. Simple and his stories began appearing in January, 1943, as part of Hughes's column for *The Chicago Defender*. Since enough of the brief stories eventually appeared to result in five collections, there are far too many stories to discuss here individually; even *The Best of Simple*, a popular selection still in print, contains over 60 stories. This chapter will therefore discuss representative stories, in ways that should shed light on the whole Simple canon; it will offer an overview of Simple's development and suggest what Simple meant to Hughes as a story writer.

Something In Common (1963), Hughes's last book of short fiction, presents the opposite problem from that of the Simple stories; because it is essentially a collection of "selected stories," much of the material it includes has been thoroughly discussed in earlier chapters. Consequently, this chapter will assess only that handful of new stories in the book.

The Genesis and Growth of Simple

Two accounts of Jesse B. Simple's birth are crucial to an understanding of what he means to Hughes's short fiction: one by Hughes himself, the other by his biographer, Arnold Rampersad.

In the Foreword to *The Best of Simple* ("Who Is Simple?"), Hughes begins essentially by saying Simple is neither fiction nor truth—the standard disclaimer of fiction writers. "The facts are," he writes, "that these tales are about a great many people—although they are stories about no specific persons as such. But it is impossible to live in Harlem and not know at least a 100 Simples, 50 Joyces, 25 Zaritas, a number of Boyds, and several Cousin Minnies—or reasonable facsimiles thereof."[12]

Although Hughes's opening statement does not get to the heart of the matter—who is Simple and how did he come to be?—it is fascinating in a couple of ways. Tellingly, Hughes uses both the words "tales" and "stories" to describe what he wrote in his column; in doing so he reveals the flexibility with which he approached the Simple narratives, and at least hints at the degree to which "folk tale" might apply to many of the pieces. Moreover, he highlights the uncertainty with which critics have approached the question of genre with regard to Simple: are these "pieces" sketches, tales, stories, "humor," columns, or what? There is no evidence, of course, that Hughes himself lost any sleep over these distinctions, but his interchangeable use of "tales" and "stories" points toward this question—it cannot really be called a problem—of genre. The critical bias of this chapter is: that since the Simple narratives are short pieces of fiction featuring conventional elements (such as character, plot, and dialogue), why not call them stories?

The opening of the foreword is useful not just because it touches on the issue of genre but also because it efficiently introduces the stable of characters, or cast, of the Simple stories: Simple himself; Boyd, by turns the narrator, the straight man, and the stand-in for Hughes; Simple's women friends, Joyce and Zarita; and Simple's Cousin Minnie, the other recurring character.

Later in the foreword, Hughes goes on to explain that Simple "sprang forth" during World War II, and that Simple's "first words" came out of the mouth of a young man Hughes encountered in a bar, presumably in Harlem. Hughes then gives this account of the meeting:

> Not knowing much about the young man, I asked where he worked. He said, "In a war plant."
> I said, "What do you make?"
> He said, "Cranks."
> I said, "What kind of cranks?"
> He said, "Oh, man, I don't know what kind of cranks."
> I said, "Well, do they crank cars, tanks, buses, planes, or what?"
> He said, "I don't know what them cranks crank."
> Whereupon, his girlfriend, a little put out at this ignorance of his job, said, "You've been working there long enough. Looks like by now you ought to know what them cranks crank."
> "Aw, woman," he said, "you know white folks don't tell colored folks what cranks crank."

"That," Hughes tells us, "was the beginning of Simple" (Foreword, viii). His account tells us both very little and very much about the origins of Simple. Characteristically, in explaining how the stories originated, Hughes chooses to tell another story—what amounts to another Simple story—choosing to tell very little about why he invented Simple and what Simple means to him. The foreword, then, represents Hughes at his most diffident, a quality that also characterizes his autobiographies, *The Big Sea* and *I Wonder As I Wander*.

In another sense, however, the story within the foreword incorporates an enormous amount of what makes the Simple stories so fascinating and deceptively original. As the encounter in the Harlem bar shows, one part of Hughes is very much a Boyd figure: an observer comfortable in Harlem but also distant, cool, aloof, and not overtly sympathetic to a "typical" Harlemite like Simple. Further, that encounter reported in the foreword shows the extent to which Hughes immediately seized on Simple's "trickster" energy: in the stories, Simple plays dumb but is remarkably shrewd; he feigns passiveness, even laziness, but is remarkably assertive, centered, and self-aware. For example, when Simple's prototype is "pushed" on the issue of cranks, his ironic answer not only justifies his alienation from his job but transforms "cranks" into a rather useful symbol of race relations, class distinctions, and mass production.

In addition, the encounter shows the extent to which wordplay ("cranks crank") is at the heart of the Simple stories; critics have variously described the origin of such play as the blues, the dozens, Vaudeville, and the African folk tradition of the Signifying Monkey, a trickster figure. What no one disputes, however, is the genius of verbal energy and linguistic deftness in the Simple stories.

And finally, the vignette within Hughes's foreword shows that however comic, jocular, and light the Simple stories may seem, they still address substantial issues of race, power, and politics. Although the fire and fierce irony of *The Ways of White Folks* no longer appeared in Hughes's fiction, a sharp edge of social criticism remained. As unmilitant, even patriotic, as Simple and his prototype could be, neither they nor Hughes lost sight of problems of race and class in the United States.

In his account of Simple's "birth," Arnold Rampersad touches on the political side of Simple:

> Why Langston should have been intrigued [by the prototype of Simple he met in the Harlem bar] at this particular moment is something of a mystery. After all, he had long recognized the power of uneducated speech in the mouths of people with little formal learning but with much to say. . . . Hughes had written semi-literate verse

(as opposed to his blues and jazz poetry) mainly to propagandize the black masses on issues such as the Spanish War and, more recently, the gravity of the threat posed by the Nazis and the Japanese. . . . Now with the same basic goal in mind—that of leading the black masses to see their destiny linked to the fate of the Allies fight against the Axis—the idea came to him that he should turn to prose. (Rampersad, II:62)

Rampersad's account of Simple's genesis in no way contradicts Hughes's; in both accounts, meeting the man in the Harlem bar amounts to a kind of revelation, an epiphany. But Rampersad's version provides additional, more complicated motives for Simple's arrival, and as Rampersad indicates, at least two of these motives were political: letting an ordinary, uneducated Harlemite speak out in his own language (the linguistic choice itself amounting to a political decision), and linking the fate of African Americans to global war. That is, one motive was political with regard to race and class consciousness, while the other was political with regard to specific world events and the role of African Americans.

As Rampersad and others have pointed out, the explicit "propagandistic" purpose behind the columns featuring Simple disappeared fairly quickly, but Simple survived and thrived. Rampersad writes: "In his first year, Simple appeared in roughly one quarter of the [*Chicago Defender*] columns. Over the following twenty-three years, as Hughes continued to fulfill his obligations to write a column for the newspaper, this proportion only increased. Simple established himself as one of the most keenly anticipated fixtures of the *Defender*, which reached black communities across the country in its national edition, and became by far the most brilliant and beloved aspect of Hughes's [column]" (Rampersad, II:64). "Simple established himself" may be the key clause of Rampersad's observations, for regardless of the particulars of his genesis, Simple took on a life of his own as no other character in Hughes's short fiction—or in any of his writing, for that matter—was to do. In Simple, Hughes found something inexhaustible and protean, an exquisite, resilient narrative vehicle—a character who always seemed to have more to reveal.

In the 23 years to which Rampersad refers, Hughes was able to perfect the art and craft of the short conversational story. The Simple stories let him comment on numerous political and social problems of the day, most of them bearing on race relations, including Jim Crow laws, the phenomenon of the "white liberal," and the emerging civil rights movement. They let him capture one crucial mode of Harlem speech, the flavor of Harlem society in the 1940s and 1950s, and the nature of gender relations in working-class African-American life.

The stories are not crude vehicles for topical comment, however; drawing on several sources, including the blues, the "dozens," vaudeville, folktales, and his own trained ear, Hughes invented a subgenre of short fiction distinctly his own. In a sense, Simple was—to use a musical analogy—a deceptively sophisticated folk instrument with which Hughes was to achieve virtuoso status.

"With tongue in cheek," writes Rampersad, "Hughes liked to pretend that there was no art whatsoever in writing the Simple columns. . . . Within a few years, however, Simple had grown into a notable Afro-American addition, without parallel in the twentieth century, to the long line of popular fictional humorists in American literature dating back several hundred years" (Rampersad, 2:65).

One additional note may be helpful before we turn to representative stories: in some of the early Simple stories and later ones in which Simple's name appears as part of a document within a story, he is referred to as Jesse B. "Semple." This latter spelling appears in a fraction of the Hughes scholarship and criticism as well. In the vast majority of stories, however, the character is "Jesse B. Simple."

Representative Jesse B. Simple Stories

As mentioned earlier, the sheer volume of Simple material dictates a selective discussion of individual stories. "Feet Live Their Own Life" is a kind of touchstone story because it was the first Simple story Hughes chose to republish in a collection (*Simple Speaks His Mind*, 1950); as a result, it deserves first mention here. In the story, Simple and Boyd banter about whether Simple's feet deserve to be seen as an emblem for his whole life. Simple claims they do; Boyd disagrees. Throughout the story, Simple maintains his bluesy, world-weary persona, by turns feeling sorry for himself, then mildly lecturing Boyd. Boyd, on the other hand, characteristically withholds his sympathy and resists Simple's philosophizing.

As in all the Simple stories, wordplay abounds, sometimes for self-contained comic effect (Simple uses "borned" for "born), more often as verbal sabotage: "'Everything I do is connected up with my past life,' said Simple. 'From Virginia to Joyce, from my wife to Zarita, from my mother's milk to this glass of beer, everything is connected up.' 'I trust you will connect up with that dollar I loaned you when you get paid,' I said."[13]

In this exchange, the wordplay and the rhetorical stances are fairly basic: Boyd undercuts Simple's philosophizing and brings the dialogue back down to earth, the planet on which Simple owes Boyd money. But even in this brief exchange, the hidden complexity of the Simple narratives can be detected. For example, while Boyd is ostensibly the smarter, more educated of the two, it is Simple who asks the larger questions of life, who "thinks big," even if he expresses himself in uneducated ways. Boyd, for all his polish, is a pedestrian thinker: quick and clever but not substantial, knowing but unadventurous.

Further, Boyd is almost an invisible first-person narrator; in a Harlem context, he plays Watson to Simple's Sherlock Holmes. Simple always dictates the subject and pace of their conversations, and he almost always gets the upper hand or at least has the last word. And finally, the short dialogues about everyday topics (feet, shoes, money) always point toward larger issues. In "Feet Live Their Own Life," for instance, Simple gives us a kind of capsule history of African Americans and their hardships in the first part of the century. Of course that is not his stated purpose, which is to talk about the history of his particular feet, the troubles only he has seen. In this sense, the Simple stories are small mirrors that nonetheless indirectly illuminate a great deal.

One important subject the Simple "canon" illuminates is gender relations. In fact, one unusual aspect of the stories is that, while they spring from dialogues between two Harlem men, Simple and Boyd, the world to which the dialogues refer is populated largely by women— Simple's wife, his girlfriends, his female relatives. (Simple, it should be noted, starts his fictional "life" married to Isabel, with Joyce and Zarita as extramarital girlfriends, Zarita being the real "party girl." Later he marries Joyce, and Zarita fades somewhat, though not altogether, from view.)

The very fact that Simple has both wives and girlfriends is in itself a comment on gender relations; adultery in Simple's world is not a shocking matter, particularly if a man commits it.

Further, in almost all of the stories that refer specifically to women, Simple presents himself as the beleaguered, henpecked male companion. As exemplified in such stories as "Jealousy" and "Summer Ain't Simple" (both collected in *Simple Speaks His Mind*, 1950), Simple also assumes he has the right to be a philanderer while his wife and other companions do not.[14] In both of these stories, he becomes possessive and puritanical when Joyce dresses a bit too stylishly for his tastes or when her eye wanders to other men. And in "Summer Ain't Simple," Simple makes it clear to Boyd he doesn't want his main girlfriend, Joyce, to dress as alluringly as his second girlfriend, Zarita; of course, he doesn't pause to reflect on the hypocrisy of his sexual principles.

It is possible to place the numerous Simple stories involving women in several contexts. First, they tell us something about the audience for the *Chicago Defender* column; clearly, Hughes wrote primarily for African-American men, though certainly not exclusively. For such an audience, "problems with women" or "girl trouble" must have seemed inexhaustible sources of comedy. Further, they reveal Hughes to be conservative on the issue of gender politics even as he was progressive, often radical, on other issues. (As both an American and African-American male writer, he is not alone in this conservative stance, of course.) That is, while his columns critique a variety of social and racial inequalities, they implicity accept double standards with regard to gender. Boyd, the Hughes "stand-in," is least adversarial with Simple in the dialogues about women.

However, without excusing or ignoring Hughes's silence on the subject of gender politics, it can be seen that the Simple stories are not so much condoning as documenting certain relationships between men and women in working-class Harlem, just as they document street language and street society. In comparison to his other political stances, Hughes remained an obdurate sexist, judging from attitudes the Simple stories reveal. (And of course the Simple stories predate the Women's Movement of the 1960s and 1970s, so the term "sexism" had not become part of the national lexicon.) Nonetheless, the stories also give us one detailed picture of gender relations in Harlem at the time and therefore operate as a form of ethnography.

One other characteristic attitude the Simple stories reveal is how persistent Hughes was, not just in advocating the inherent worth of African-American culture (such as the blues and jazz), but in resisting attempts to make it exotic or academic.

In "Jazz, Jive, and Jam," for instance, Simple reports to Boyd concerning a lecture he and Joyce attended—given, he says, by a "Negro hysterian." Joyce thinks the lecture is wonderful; Simple thinks it is not only just dry but off the mark: "Joyce said, 'This was a serious seminar, aiming at facts, not fun.' 'Baby,' I said, 'what is more facts than acts? Jazz makes people get into action, move! Didn't nobody move in that hall where you were—except to jerk their head up when they went to sleep, to keep anybody from seeing that they was nodding. . . .'"[15]

Here Simple—and Hughes—advocate the living, organic, performance-oriented aspect of jazz and resist attempts, even by historians who happen to be black, to over-intellectualize it—to freeze and study it out of a performance context. And of course, because the entire Simple canon springs from and honors the performance aspects of Harlem conversation as a kind of public art form, the story, in a way, bears on literature with folk roots as well.

The issue of popular African-American culture becomes more complicated in stories like "The Blues" (*Simple's Uncle Sam*), in which Simple laments that "young folks" prefer rock and roll to the blues.[16] On the one hand, the lament makes Simple seem to take the old-fashioned side of a generation gap, but on the other, it obliquely raises the question of rock and roll's debt to the blues and the extent to which white artists, agents, and record executives have exploited black songwriters and performers. ("Rock and Roll is seventy-two-and-one-half per cent blues," remarks Simple.) Mainly, however, Simple and Hughes prefer the blues because the blues are more complicated than rock and roll: "But it [Rock and Roll] don't have so many different kinds of expressions as does the blues! The blues can be real sad, else real mad, else real glad, and funny, too, all at the same time" ("The Blues," 17).

In any event, on the subject of the blues and jazz, the Simple stories reveal how unwaveringly Hughes remained committed to grassroots African-American culture and loyal to a literary ethos expressed in the essay "The Negro Artist and the Racial Mountain," which he published in 1926 and which is discussed in detail in part 2 of this book.

Of course, the most obvious and expansive subject to which the Simple stories refer is race relations in the United States. Like the characters Cora or Berry in *The Ways of White Folks* or Sargeant in *Laughing To Keep From Crying*, Simple is a witness to those relations. Because of his Virginia past, Simple is able to comment on Jim Crow laws, lynching, slavery, and other topics; because of his Harlem present, he is able to comment on economic injustice, urban riots, the phenomenon of the ghetto, and numerous northern manifestations of racism.

That Hughes could address such topics in short conversational stories without seeming reductive or trivial is another testament to his subtle narrative art. A story like "Adventure" shows the tightrope Hughes had to walk when writing comically about race relations.[17]

In this story, Simple archly suggests that if people, particularly young white people, seek adventure, they should go down South as Freedom Riders: "If I had a son I wanted to make a man out of, I would send him to Jackson, Mississippi, or Selma, Alabama—and not in a covered wagon, but on a bus. Especially if he was a white boy. . . ." ("Adventure," 66).

Simple goes on to explore the analogy between the "wild West" of yore and the "savage South" of the late 1950s and early 1960s. The analogy is a biting one, implying the real savages of American history aren't the Indians of yesterday but the racists of today. And as Simple explores the analogy further, it becomes clear that Hughes is casting a cold eye toward white counterculture youth: "'That is why the South will make a man of you, my son,' I would say. 'Go South, baby, go South. Let a fiery cross singe the beard off your beatnik chin. Let Mississippi make a man out of you" ("Adventure," 67). The implicit criticism here seems to be that the quarrel the Beats and their imitators have with mainstream society shrinks in comparison to the complaint blacks still have with that society, especially in the South. If one pushes the critique even further, Hughes may be suggesting that counterculture white youth fail to realize the position of privilege from which they resist the established culture. It is a point that would not have been lost on the chief readership of the *Chicago Defender*.

In "Duty Is Not Snooty" (*The Best of Simple*), Hughes tests white liberalism further. In this story, Simple suggests that "if white people who say they love Negroes really do love them, then they ought to live like Negroes live"—by going to the South to live under Jim Crow laws.[18] After he and Boyd quibble about the idea for a while, Simple says,

> "'It [going South to live like Negroes] would teach them how dumb it is to have WHITE and COLORED signs all over Dixie.'
> Boyd replies,
> 'Liberal whites already agree that is stupid.'
> 'They would agree more if they experienced it.'"

Boyd then admits he could not bring himself to live under Jim Crow laws. "Neither would I," says Simple. "Then you would not be very good, either," proclaims Boyd. "No," says Simple, "but I would be white" ("Duty," 198).

To a greater extent even than "Adventure," "Duty Is Not Snooty" shows the way in which Hughes viewed several sides of "the race question." He looked at the obvious injustices and brutalities, but also cast a cold eye at those who seemed to want to help. Just as he was wary of the whites who wanted to "experience" Harlem in the 1920s because it was "exotic," he was wary of whites who wanted to join the cause of Civil Rights in the 1950s, feeling perhaps that many of them, in love with an idea of "the Negro" or "freedom," were still operating out of self-interest and from an enormous psychic, historical, and economic distance.

If "Duty Is Not Snooty" tells us something of Hughes's politics and his attitude toward white liberals, it also reflects the kind of writer he was. In everything he wrote, there is a grounded, reportorial, documentary side, an insistence on authenticity of place, language, and material. Hughes, in this regard at least, always came clean with himself and did not pretend to know more than he did or fake anything in his poetry, fiction, essays, or drama. This loyalty to authenticity is connected to his use of the blues, jazz, and other popular or folk material. It also influences his politics, however, for implicit in a story like "Duty Is Not Snooty" is the suspicion that the white liberal conception of "the Negro" is inauthentic, insincere, and ultimately as destructive as overt racism.

There are unexpected moments in the Simple stories when Boyd briefly steps forward, becoming more than Simple's straight man and the voice of dour common sense, reflecting something of the muted lyricism to be found in Hughes's poetry. For example, the story "The Seven Rings" begins with this monologue from Boyd: "Early blue evening. The street lights had just come on, large watery moonstones up and down the curbs. April. The days were stretching leisurely. This particular evening had become too old to eat dinner and too young to do much of anything else. It was unseasonably warm. Tasting spring, Harlem relaxed. Windows, stoops, and streets full of people not doing anything much. In spite of his landlady's request *not* to sit on the steps in front of her house, Simple was sitting there."[19]

At this point, the story slips quickly into the accustomed Simple/Boyd dialogue and takes up more of Simple's "woman trouble"; but the lyrical opening shows the extent to which Boyd is, in his own way, as much a denizen of Harlem as Simple is. It also enhances one's sense of the Simple stories as an extended celebration of Harlem.

Simple's own particular celebration of Harlem occurs most explicitly in "A Toast to Harlem," as evidenced in this exchange midway through the story (Boyd speaks first):

> "Harlem has a few Negro leaders," I said. "Elected by my *own* vote,"
> said Simple. "Here I ain't scared to vote—that's another thing I like

about Harlem. I also like it because we've got subways and it does not take all day to get downtown, neither are you Jim Crowed on the way. . . . Sometimes I run into Duke Ellington on 125th Street and I say, 'What you know there, Duke? Duke says, 'Solid, ole man.' He does not know me from Adam, but he speaks. One day I saw Lena Horne coming out of the Hotel Theresa and I said, 'Hubba! Hubba!' Lena smiled. Folks is friendly in Harlem. I feel like I got the world in a jug and the stopper in my hand! So drink a toast to Harlem!"[20]

As always, out of Simple's garrulousness emerges a surprisingly complicated portrait of Harlem—a portrait of what it is (friendly, busy, black), but also of what it is not (pretentious). Also, Simple's toast contains echoes of Harlem as Hughes had seen it decades earlier, when jazz first ascended the throne of popular culture in New York City.

As the national politics of race intensified during the 1950s, the Simple stories reflected how Harlem became a much more complicated place in which to live, a site of enormous tension. In one of the least comic, most urgent stories, "American Dilemma," Hughes, through Simple, links Harlem and Birmingham. To begin the story, Simple reports that the night before, walking the streets, he has run into a white policeman and almost said, "Birmingham." This exchange with Boyd follows:

> "Seemingly, then, you equate all white people with the brutalities of Birmingham, even whites in New York."
> "I do," said Simple. "After dark, Harlem is black, except for cops. Here of lately, it looks like there is more white cops than ever strolling around our corners at night. They must be expecting more trouble."
> "What 'they'?" I asked.
> "The white folks downtown."[21]

Simple goes on to say he almost feels sorry for the white policeman because he is a pawn of municipal racial politics.

Even within the established limits of a comic, conversational mode, then, Hughes could show the extent to which racial politics were changing, and the extent to which New York and other cities were becoming increasingly divided along racial lines. Contrasted with "American Dilemma," Simple's "Toast to Harlem" reads like a eulogy for a Harlem of the past, a Harlem that was more cultural sanctuary, less an armed camp. Also, "American Dilemma" reflects the political urgency that drove

Hughes's very first collection of stories; in the Simple stories, Hughes is still recording, commenting on, and analyzing "the ways of white folks."

Simple in the Development of Hughes's Short Fiction

What did Simple mean to Hughes the short-story writer? To some extent, the character allowed him to blend successfully the social critique that characterized *The Ways of White Folks* and the comic vein that characterized *Laughing To Keep From Crying*. Further, the short, conversational form, dictated, in part, by the limits of a newspaper column, allowed him to realize new dimensions of vernacular narrative: fiction that drew heavily on the blues, the "dozens," the street talk of Harlem, and a broad-based African-American oral tradition. As Arnold Rampersad has suggested, Simple also let Hughes integrate two aspects of his own personality—the garrulous, folksy, sociable side (Simple), and the reserved, diffident, solitary, educated side (Boyd).

In a sense, Simple did not grow immensely during his 23 years and hundreds of stories: in part because he seemed to spring whole into Hughes's imagination in 1943, and in part because the Simple/Boyd "routine" is static the way Vaudeville acts are static. Simple had a prescribed role to play within the stories. But Hughes made sure Simple stayed aware of the changing times, and in this sense there is a suppleness and flexibility to the Simple canon. To contrast "A Toast to Harlem" with "American Dilemma," as this chapter has done, reveals that suppleness, that eye toward a changing history.

To a large extent, Simple allowed Hughes to continue to map out a territory within short fiction far removed from the one defined by the modernists. It is a territory inspired by Carl Sandburg and his regard for the common person, by D. H. Lawrence and his regard for both the working class and direct, bracing literature, and by several strains of African-American culture, including the blues and folk tales. And it was certainly a territory that allowed him to celebrate the resilience of African Americans, for Simple is above all a survivor, as critic Eugenia Collier notes in her study of Simple as an epic hero: "An epic hero embodies the values of a culture. Simple is the ideal black folk hero. His name, Jesse B. Simple, implies the ruse which has enabled the folk black man to survive. Also, and more significantly, it implies the direct way in which Simple confronts life, without phoniness and false expectations. . . . He is a wise man: his logic is perfect. If his statements seem humorous and incongruous, we soon realize that it is our culture that is out of tune."[22]

With regard to the audience for short fiction, Simple allowed Hughes to break new ground. Whereas most of the stories collected in *The Ways of White Folks* and *Laughing To Keep From Crying* had their publishing origins in mainstream, middle-class magazines with predominantly white readerships, the Simple stories appeared in a newspaper with a predominantly black readership. Perhaps even more than in Hughes's poetry and drama, then, the Simple stories enabled Hughes to fulfill one goal expressed in his manifesto "The Negro Artist and the Racial Mountain": to speak to, for, and about working-class African Americans. James Emanuel comments on this common-person aspect of Hughes's short fiction and his life: "Traveling throughout the world, Langston Hughes was always a man of the people, equally at home eating camel sausage in an Asian desert or tasting strawberries in a Park Avenue penthouse. He once said that he lived much of his life in basements and attics. Metaphorically, his realism and his humanity derive from this fact. . . . At the same time, writing in attics like the one he occupied in Harlem for twenty years, he rose to the long perspective that enabled him to shine a humanizing, beautifying, but still truthful light on what he saw."[23]

In the way Emanuel characterizes him, Hughes the short-story writer went against the grain of modern American short fiction. After World War II, when the readership for the short story was shrinking, and short-story writers increasingly gravitated toward universities for employment and small presses for publication, Hughes continued to sustain himself through his writing and to write for a nonacademic audience. His longstanding affinity for the common person, then, applied both to the contents and audience of the Simple stories.

Contrasted with the protagonists that would populate African-American fiction in the 1950s, 1960s and 1970s, the Simple stories show Hughes also going against the grain. The heroes of Ralph Ellison's, James Baldwin's, and Ishmael Reed's fiction, for example, are often much more alienated and enraged than Simple. Although Hughes's politics remained quite similar to that of younger writers, this choice of protagonist may have seemed old-fashioned, an echo of an older Harlem. To probe Simple the character is to find out that he is surprisingly militant and "with it," and that Hughes is politically astute; nonetheless, Simple's appeal is much different from that of Ellison's invisible man or the main characters in Baldwin's *Go Tell It On The Mountain, Tell Me How*

Long The Train's Been Gone, and other fictions. Simple certainly was not the antithesis of the emerging Black Aesthetic, an aesthetic for which Hughes helped pave the way, but neither was he its clear fulfillment. Simple, like his creator Hughes, was something of an anomaly, a loner on the landscape of African-American literature after World War II.

It is easy to overlook or underestimate Simple, not just because he is a loner in this sense, but also because he is only one part of Hughes's intricate, multifaceted literary output. Simple can get lost among the abundance of the poetry, the essays, the drama, and the connection to the Harlem Renaissance. But to look closely at Simple is to recognize a completely original comic figure in American literature; an exquisite achievement in the brief, conversational, improvised mode of short fiction; a remarkable artistic vehicle for social and political commentary; and a character with as much appeal to everyday newspaper readers as to experienced readers of short fiction. In these ways, Simple is an astounding achievement, comparable to any recurring character one can think of in short fiction, American or otherwise.

Because Simple is a recurring character, he possesses both idiosyncratic and mythic/typical/Everyman characteristics. Blyden Jackson has intelligently examined both sides of Simple. He writes: "[Simple] represents a great departure from the stereotypes of the Negro traditionally afloat in the common lore of the American mass intelligence. He is not Little Black Sambo grown up and existing half-wittedly in an urban setting beyond his resources to cope with, nor is he a brute, a demented apeman with a fearful affinity for lust and pillage, especially apropos the bodies and properties of persons more Nordic than himself. . . . Thus, in Hughes's warm and sane definition of an average Negro, Simple is no freak of any kind."[24]

Hughes set out to explore a type of African-American man, fusing this Harlem Everyman with elements of literary, stage, and oral types: the wise naif, the wordplay expert, Uncle John from slave tales. While he was constructing Simple, however, Hughes was also deconstructing other typical images of the African-American male, as Jackson suggests. So if Hughes was holding up a mirror to urban, working-class African-American men, he was also smashing the false images of "the Negro" which white society had created.

Something in Common and Other Stories

This, Hughes's last short-fiction collection, contains only 10 stories not previously collected. It appeared in 1963.[25]

"The Gun" manages to be both a quirky and representative Hughes story. To a degree, it calls to mind one of Hughes's earliest and most successful stories, "Cora Unashamed," because it involves a lone black woman, Flora Belle Yates of Tall Rock, Montana, in a small American town. Her parents, she learns, have fled Texarkana one violent night, a lynch mob at their heels. (The similarity of the names, Flora/Cora, seems more than coincidental.)

Unlike Cora, however, Flora does not remain in Tall Rock to discover and live out the fate of the town's only black child. Instead she hits the roads of the West Coast, exhibiting some of the wanderlust of Hughes himself. She careens from Butte to Seattle, "where folks is so cold and it rains all the time" (*Something in Common*, 158) and from Seattle to Monterey, Berkeley, San Diego, Marysville, San Jose, and finally Fresno. Along the way she works as a servant to white families and to "rich Mexicans" (p. 159).

Much of the story, then, recapitulates material common to Hughes's short fiction: the plight of an isolated African-American working-class person; someone "on the move," out of necessity more than out of choice; a brisk, spare, plot-driven narrative. When Flora hits Fresno, though, the story takes its quirky, uncharacteristic turn.

In Fresno, Flora's incapacity to feel at home anywhere drives her to suicidal thoughts (p. 159). She buys a pistol, loads it, and goes so far as to put the barrel to her chest: "Then she put the pistol down, undressed, and went to bed. Somehow she felt better, as though she could go off anytime now to some sweet good place, as though she were no longer a prisoner in the world, or in herself" (*Something in Common*, 160). The potential instrument of her suicide becomes—outlandishly, perversely, but somehow believably—an instrument of survival. Subsequently, Flora falls in love with the pistol.

This plot twist adds both absurd, Kafkaesque and gothic, Faulknerian elements to the story: Flora has a bit of both Gregor Samsa and Miss Emily Grierson about her. At the end of the story, she is at once pathetic, ludicrous, and sympathetic. Driven to madness, Flora finds a way to control her destiny, as the last sentence suggests: "She is still living alone over the white folks' garage in Fresno—but now she can go away anytime she wants to" (161). So while the character and situation seem at first familiar, Hughes's use of symbolic device and the absurd twist make "The Gun" an altogether refreshing, unexpected addition to the collection.

"Sorrow For A Midget" is not as successful as "The Gun," but in it Hughes works with more quasi-absurd, quasi-gothic material. The story is narrated by a familiar Hughes character, a no-nonsense man who has landed a job as an orderly in a hospital: "I was broke, jobs hard to find, and the employment office sent me there that winter" (*Something in Common*, 143). In the hospital is " a little lady who looked like a dried-up child" to the narrator; he calls her "Countess Midget," and she pays him cash out of her pocket to take special care of her. She is in the hospital to die.

She claims she has a son, and indeed, a man claiming to be her son shows up. He is down on his luck and tells her he regrets not being a better child; she forgives him and tells him, "You have been my *only* son" (146). Subsequently, the narrator finds out the man was her adopted son.

Like "The Gun," then, "Sorrow For a Midget" combines some familiar elements—economic hard times, an unsentimental narrator, and strained family relations, for instance—with a less familiar, more gothic, freakish situation. The story, convincing us how much Hughes was drawn to the situation, even draws us into the situation, but in the end brings the characters on stage without letting them fulfill the drama. It appears that Hughes did not quite figure out precisely where the situation should lead.

"Early Autumn" is a shorter, slighter story than "Sorrow For A Midget," but within its own limits is more fully realized. It is an "urban encounter" story in which former lovers meet on a street corner, exchange pleasantries, pretend to care for one another, but finally decide, without saying as much, to bury the past: "The bus started. People came between them outside, people crossing the street, people they didn't know. Space and people. She lost sight of Bill. Then she remembered she had forgotten to give him her address—or to ask him for his—or tell him that her youngest boy was named Bill, too" (*Something in Common*, 190).

Although the last line adds a bit of a twist to the story, in the main, the narrative is a lyrical but unsentimental study of lost intimacy; outside of the Simple stories, it ranks with "Saratoga Rain" as one of Hughes's most successful short-short stories.

"His Last Affair" recapitulates many of the psychosexual themes through which Hughes examined racism in his early short stories, and contains echoes of "A Good Job Gone," "Cora Unashamed," and "Red-Headed Baby." In it, a wealthy midwestern business man visits New York, runs into a former lover from "the wrong side of town," from Terre Haute, and pursues a last tryst with her. We discover that she had become pregnant by him in their younger days but that his parents paid her mother to keep the matter quiet. After the tryst in New York he returns to Terre Haute, and the woman calls him to blackmail him, claiming again to be "with child" (*Something in Common*, 100). We now discover that in neither instance was the woman really pregnant and that the businessman is unaware she has been "passing" as a white woman.

The elements of race, class, and sexual exploitation seem tired and worn in this story, not because they have suddenly become irrelevant, but perhaps because Hughes seems to have no real affinity for any of the characters. "His Last Affair" seems to be a narrative that needed to be pushed toward satire and comedy—like "Rejuvenation Through Joy," for instance—to be successful; left as straight drama, it runs out of energy. By contrast, the story demonstrates how successfully and powerfully Hughes handled similar material in *The Ways of White Folks*.

"No Place to Make Love," as sly a narrative as "His Last Affair," is less obvious and forced. It is a monologue spoken by a poor young man; Hughes takes pains to insure that we know the narrator is poorly educated, almost a simpleton. Because the man and his lover have "no place to make love," they get married and quickly have several children. Toward the end of the story, the monologue "turns" to reveal a specific listener within the story: "You're the second welfare investigator what's been here. The first one, the white man, said he couldn't do a thing. . . . We got rent to pay. We don't want our kid to be born out in the cold, maybe growing up like we did—without even a place to make love. I don't want relief, Mister, but I do want a job. I know you understand. You niggers have a hard time, too, don't you?" (*Something In Common*, 169).

This elegant turn in the story allows Hughes to achieve a great deal. He shatters the stereotype of "the welfare family" being black; he shows the maddening contradictions of the narrator, who recognizes, on the one hand, that economic strife cuts across racial boundaries, but then, on the other hand, insults the case worker with a racist epithet. The story also allows Hughes to explore a different kind of situational irony springing from racial conflict—namely, that working-poor white Americans may, for the first time in their lives, be confronted with blacks who are not just above them on the ladder of American class, but who also work in a "welfare" profession designed to insure more social justice. In this story, Hughes does not fully probe the disorienting effects of such relatively new social situations, but with his clever choice of narrative point of view, suggests such disorientation quite well.

"Breakfast in Virginia" and "Fine Accommodations," two "train" stories, also involve awkward social situations and the seemingly endless transitions "race relations" pass through in the United States. In "Breakfast in Virginia," two "colored" [*sic*] soldiers travel during World War II from a Southern training camp to Harlem; one is a Southerner who's never been North, the other a native of New York. They have to travel in the Jim Crow car until the train reaches Washington. An older white man, seeing they are soldiers, invites them to dine with him, but they are refused service in the dining car. The white man then invites them to dine with him in his private car; they accept the invitation.

At least two crucial themes or subtexts emerge from this vignette. First, Hughes makes it clear that African Americans can serve their nation in war but still be regarded as second-class citizens; second, he seems to hint that, at least for some southern whites, patriotism outweighs racism: the southern gentleman is moved to invite the soldiers to his compartment because they are soldiers. For Hughes, as for most Americans, World War II complicated matters of race at home, but the complications were not necessarily negative, as "Breakfast in Virginia" suggests in its measured way.

"Fine Accommodations," which takes place on a train traveling from Atlanta to Washington, chiefly involves a conversation between a black porter and a black professor; the latter serves as a secretary for and is traveling with the black president of a southern "Negro" college. The porter tells the professor he wants to send his son to the college, but the professor warns him against it, saying his boss, the president, is a patsy for the powers that be in Washington and that the southern white trustees of the school still want blacks to remain powerless.

At the end of the story, the black college president returns to the compartment and asks the professor if he has finished copying a report. "'Yes,' said the young man, 'but I didn't agree with it.' 'It's not necessary that you agree,' snapped Dr. Jenkins as the porter went out. The rest of the words were lost as the door closed and the train roared through the night. For a moment the porter stood thinking in the corridor. 'The last Negro passenger I had in that drawing room was a pimp from Birmingham. Now I got a professor. I guess both of them have to have ways of paying for such fine accommodations'" (*Something In Common*, 166).

To some extent, in "Fine Accommodations" Hughes is his old fierce self, indicting the hypocrisy of some Negro colleges, contrasting a professor who swallows his outrage to a pimp. And as usual, it is the working-class porter who gets the last word and remains unsullied.

Especially when contrasted with "Breakfast in Virginia," this story, focusing on the connection between race and class, seems to be a throwback to the stories in *The Ways of White Folks*.

"Blessed Assurance" and "Rock, Church" both allow Hughes to return to his love/hate relationship with organized religion; he seems to love the ambience of "church" but cannot resist pointing out the hypocrisy of some organized religion. "Rock Church" describes the rise and fall of an overly ambitious minister, Elder William Jones, who was "too ambitious. He wouldn't let well enough alone. He wanted to be a big shot and panic Harlem, gas Detroit, sew up Chicago, then move to Hollywood. He wasn't satisfied with just St. Louis" (*Something in Common*, 15). The story is Hughes's chance to satirize self-serving evangelists.

"Blessed Assurance" is more complicated because it involves homosexuality. The story is told through the point of view of John, who fears that his son is gay. Hughes uses the word "queer." The son is a talented singer, but he sounds like a woman. John is mortified when he hears his son sing beautifully in church. The story is fascinating in part because Hughes seems unsure about how to let the story play out. To some extent, he seems to want to ask rhetorically whether homosexuals are welcome in church and to show that John's son, for example, is in some sense blessed by God. But in the end, Hughes turns the story into little more than an elaborate joke on John and comes close to stereotyping homosexuals as effeminate and girlish. Hughes's own ambivalence about his sexuality is well known, and it is a subject Arnold Rampersad discusses frequently in his two-volume *Life* of Hughes. The biographical background does not necessarily account for or explain the unevenness of "Blessed Assurance," of course, but the tentativeness with which Hughes handles the convergence of sexuality and religion is in itself interesting.

"Gumption" is another of Hughes's monologue stories, spoken by an elderly black woman who is angry with the younger generation of her family for being whiners, for not knowing how hard things were for her generation, and for having no "gumption": "You young folks don't remember the depression, but I do. No jobs for nobody" (*Something In Common*, 67).

The story is clearly an opportunity for Hughes to chide younger blacks and to recall just how harsh the Great Depression was. It is an immensely playful story, however, not a boring retreat into the past or a lament for the Harlem Renaissance, which in effect was crushed by the depression. It is also a kind of tribute to the working women of Hughes's generation.

None of the previously uncollected stories in *Something In Common* rival the achievement of his best stories from the 1930s, or his most memorable Simple stories; none are Hughes classics. They reveal instead how comfortable he had become with the kind of vignette story that relies upon dialogue and with the brief monologue. They also reveal how concerned he remained with issues of social injustice, and how sharp his eye still was for confluences of race and class in the United States.

Character Types and Narrative Modes

The first three chapters in part 1 have analyzed Hughes's short fiction in roughly chronological order, evaluating and interpreting his first two collections, analyzing his original achievement in the Simple stories, and discussing how his narrative art changed over time. These chapters noted, among other things, the influence of D. H. Lawrence on the ethos of *The Ways of White Folks,* the experience and maturity Hughes brought to short fiction, having already published extensively, and the shift in temperament that seems to have taken place in *Laughing To Keep From Crying* and the Simple stories—a shift away from the fierce, sometimes embittered social critique of the first collection toward a wryer but by no means less socially alert perspective.

One other especially productive way to approach Hughes's stories is to take a cross section of them, focusing on the kinds of characters with which Hughes was preoccupied and on key narrative modes he employed in short fiction.

Powerless Characters

Because Hughes dedicated himself to grounding literary art in authentic African-American experience and because both race and class consciousness informs his writing, as a short-story writer he is a voice for the powerless. To a great degree, his stories speak for those who are disenfranchised, cheated, abused, or ignored because of race or class (usually both). In his first collection, after all, "the ways of white folks" his stories illuminate are the ways in which white folks exert power over black folks.

Although his stories are filled with characters who are significantly powerless, the nature of the powerlessness and the ways in which power is negotiated differ substantially from story to story. In particular, at least three kinds of powerless characters seem to emerge: victims, survivors, and rebels.

In one sense, most of Hughes's characters are victims, at least in the sense that they must deal with racism in one way or another; they are all victims of American history.

But more specific kinds of victims, characters overwhelmed or destroyed by particular manifestations of power, take shape dramatically in *The Ways of White Folks*. Indeed, as noted in chapter 1, an implicit guiding principle of that collection seems to have been to tell the brutal truth about race relationships in the United States.

The purest victim in all of Hughes's stories may well be Roy Williams of the story "Home" in *The Ways of White Folks* (32–48). He is the ailing jazz musician who tours Europe, returns to his hometown in Missouri, and is lynched because he tips his hat to a white woman. One purpose of the story is unadorned and direct: black men get lynched in America, the story reminds its readers, because of the psychosexual dimensions of racism in America, dimensions "white America" refuses to confront.

In less obvious terms, however, Roy Williams is lynched because he is a witness. The whole first third of the story is taken up with his observations of Europe and America in the midst of the Great Depression. He sees people starving in Vienna and believes they have it even worse than African Americans back in the States. When he returns to the States, he arrives on the day President Hoover drives the World War I veterans from their tent city in Washington D.C. This part of the story reveals the extent to which Hughes's critique is both "economic" (focused on poverty, capital, class) and racial. The story suggests one way in which rough economic times only enhance preexisting racism to create more opportunities for scapegoating and violence.

As a quiet, reflective, nonviolent jazz musician, Roy Williams is not a martyr in a grandiose, melodramatic, or highly politicized way. He is an unassuming man, a loner, an artist. From almost any perspective except a violently irrational and racist one, he is absolutely no threat to anyone. Consequently, Hughes demonstrates the way in which racism is projection: Williams' lynchers do not see him; they see only the objectified "Negro" in their minds. Against the fury of such projection, Roy Williams is powerless.

Although other Hughes characters encounter less violent treatment than Roy Williams, they exhibit a similar powerlessness; this is particularly true of certain children, such as those in "Red-Headed Baby" and "African Morning." In both stories, these mulatto offspring become at once products and victims of racial conflict and economic oppression. Whereas in a story like "Passing" Hughes explored the dubious power and freedom of being a mulatto who could pass as white, in these stories the children are cast aside. They fail from the outset to pass. And in both stories, Hughes shows how such illegitimate children become objects, rather than people, in the eyes of those who behold them. The red-headed baby becomes nothing more than a circus doll to her alcoholic father; the child in "African Morning" becomes a kind of gold coin. The powerlessness that springs from being of mixed race in a society that is racist therefore results in objectification. These stories suggest the process is almost as dehumanizing as lynching, if less obviously so.

Many other characters in Hughes's short fiction encounter implacable white power, including the main characters of "Cora Unashamed" and "Berry" in *The Ways of White Folks*; but the jazz musician Roy Williams and the two mulatto children represent the ultimate destructive consequences of racism, in part because they have nothing with which to struggle against it.

In other stories, however, Hughes shows survival itself to be resistance. Many—not all—of the survivors show up in the comic stories. For example, "On the Road" (from *Laughing To Keep From Crying*) is in one sense a satire on institutionalized Christianity, but in another sense is a parable for survival. Like Roy Williams and the mulatto children, Sargeant is driven to extremes; he is freezing and starving to death, and ends up in jail. But while he is defeated, he is not destroyed, nor is he objectified or dehumanized as Williams and the children are in the stories just discussed. In fact, Sargeant's innocent goodwill becomes a powerful indictment of institutionalized religion, and jail is not depicted as the end of the road for him.

Throughout Hughes's books of fiction there are characters who, like Sargeant, exist at the periphery of economic and social power and, as in the blues songs, laugh to keep from crying. To a great extent, Jesse B. Simple is the apotheosis of this type of character. As an ordinary denizen of Harlem, Simple does not wield enormous economic, political, or artistic power. But as a folk philosopher and trickster, he turns his "ordinariness" into power. His being ordinary gives him a kind of authority that the better-educated Boyd, for example, does not have; he is always reminding Boyd—and us—of "where he's been." Indeed, one of the earliest and best-known Simple stories, "Feet Live Their Own Life," constitutes Simple's journey over the rocky, often racist, American landscape. Furthermore, we come to see his simplicity as a kind of trickster's mask, especially when we see how verbally adept and personally resilient he is. His simplicity is that of the sly fox. In any event, he is Hughes's Great Survivor, an urban hero and a prince of the powerless.

The victims and survivors who populate Hughes's stories remind us that, temperamentally and politically, Hughes focused his vision on the circumstances and consequences of "the race question" in the United States. Throughout all this short fiction beginning with *The Ways of White Folks*, his stories show a determination to document inequity and to tell the tales of the voiceless multitudes who must negotiate inequity. Rarely did Hughes shift his focus from circumstances and consequences to reform or revolution. Considering how political he was and how attractive class-oriented social theories were to him, this is, to some degree, a surprise. In a couple of memorable instances, however, stories such as "The Blues I'm Playing" and "Father and Son," portray fierce resistance. In "The Blues I'm Playing," the "revolution" is not overt, violent, or even political, in the way these terms are customarily used; it is personal and artistic, but no less effective or momentous for being so. And in a broader connotation of the term, it is most "political" indeed.

Oceola Jones, the talented African-American pianist nurtured by a white, wealthy patron, turns her back on patronage and "High Culture" to embrace the blues and her African heritage. Her gesture is unsensational: she simply plays the blues for her patron when the blues is the last thing the patron wants to hear. Consequently, the "rebellion" in this instance is quintessentially Hughesian: it is quiet yet determined, unassuming yet relentless. By playing the song, Oceola says, in effect, "I *will* be who I am" in the face of everyone, including the wealthy white who suggests she should change.

Of all the characters in *The Ways of White Folks*, Oceola emerges as the one most whole at the end of "her" story. Other characters emerge physically whole, and others are by no means emotionally obliterated, but Oceola actually flourishes by means of resistance. Perhaps the character in "Passing" offers the most instructive contrast in this regard. He has negotiated power successfully by passing as white and moving into the mainstream economy, but as his letter to his mother suggests, he has done so at the expense of his family. In public he must deny his heritage. Physically and economically, he is "all right," but he suffers the consequences of racism internally.

Oceola, in direct contrast, casts off the accountrements of assimilation—patronage, musical training, socializing with whites—and embraces her heritage. At the end of her story, we sense her journey may well be economically uncertain without the patronage, but do not doubt she will thrive as a musician and a person.

On many levels, the story of Oceola's gentle but firm rebellion is a tale of self-assertion and of identity claimed. By playing the blues, she embraces the blues; she asserts the value of African-American art. By turning away from patronage, she shows control and a narrow definition of culture and self. And by living her own life, which is in part living with the black man of whom the patron disapproves, she asserts a sexual and emotional identity as well.

In "The Blues I'm Playing," then, we are able to see the extent to which personal identity melds with racial identity, and the extent to which art melds with politics. All of these elements converge when Oceola plays her blues anthem at the story's climax. In this case, survival becomes triumph; artistically, personally, and politically, Oceola prevails as no other character does in *The Ways of White Folks*. It would be a mistake, of course, to read "The Blues I'm Playing" as thinly-veiled autobiography, but the connections between Oceola's story and Hughes's journey as a writer only enhance our understanding of the story. Hughes struggled against both a disapproving father and a narrow-minded patron, and in both literal and figurative ways, his artistic quest was to honor and embrace the blues as a kind of emblem for African-American cultural heritage.

Hughes's fiercest story of rebellion, "Father and Son," is also, in part, a tale of identity. The mulatto Bert returns to his white father's plantation to force his father to acknowledge him. As many critics have noted, "Father and Son" is Hughes's most classically tragic, bloody, and "Faulknerian" story. In the context of all Hughes's stories, not just of *The Ways of White Folks*, "Father and Son" stands alone as the apocalyptic fiction that most prefigures James Baldwin's essays and novels, such as *The Fire Next Time* or *Tell Me How Long the Train's Been Gone*.

As with the lynching story, "Home," "Father and Son" shows us that unadulterated violence is and may continue to be one result of America's failure to confront its racial problems in their numerous manifestations, indeed, "Father and Son" creates a kind of myth of confrontation. By saying, in effect, This is who I am, your black son, Bert is also saying to Colonel Norwood, This is who you are, who we are.

In essence, "Father and Son" as a story of rebellion is the violent opposite of "The Blues I'm Playing." The latter is a story full of possibility, healthy self-assertion, and cultural independence. The former is a story of denial, self-destruction, and cultural negation. Clearly, Hughes presents the vision of "Father and Son" as one terrible possibility, for in the end Bert is lynched.

It is significant, too, that both stories are in part stories of family rebellion: in "The Blues I'm Playing," Oceola's patron is a kind of surrogate parent, a controlling, stifling "mother" Oceola cannot abide.

And in "Father and Son," the hideous paradox is that Bert must slay his father to gain his father's acknowledgment, must act out the most extreme scenario of rebellion in order to be accepted. In these stories, at least, Hughes dramatizes a kind of sick pseudofamilial relationship between whites and blacks in America; his vision here is by no means particularly Freudian or Jungian, but he does illuminate a powerful psychological dimension of social, economic, and artistic conflicts.

To some extent, Hughes's short fiction continually provides narrative "answers" to the question, "How do African Americans survive and thrive in the maelstrom of white power?" From "Cora Unashamed" through the "urban folktales" of Jesse B. Simple, Hughes is preoccupied with victims, survivors, rebels, assimilators, and loners. Sometimes they are obliterated by power, but more often they manage to deflect it and define and assert their own power. As the characters Oceola Jones and Jesse B. Simple (to name two of many) demonstrate, simply asserting one's identity and claiming one's heritage is often the most powerful weapon. It is in being themselves that Oceola and Simple define and protect their niche and thereby begin to erode the monolith of racism.

Narrative Modes

One premise of this study is that Hughes's stories implicitly define a kind of story that is different from modernist modes crafted by James Joyce, Katherine Mansfield, Ernest Hemingway, and others. In this as in other matters, Hughes was something of an anomaly; he was an "old-fashioned innovator." He was old-fashioned in the sense that he was drawn to the story-as-tale or the story-as-sketch and preferred a style less polished and less elliptical than that of most modernists. (Sherwood Anderson's review of *The Ways of White Folks*, discussed in detail in part 3, helps sharpen the difference between Hughes and the chief modernist story writers.) But he was an innovator in the way he boldly handled issues of race and class in short fiction, made use of an oral tradition, and especially in the way he developed the very brief, dialogue-dependent Simple stories.

Examining a cross section of the narrative modes within Hughes's short fiction, at least three main forms emerge: the traditional dramatic story with a clear plot, conflict, and resolution; the sketch, with a journalistic or nonfiction texture and muted dramatic action; and the "oral" story, heavily dependent on monologue and dialogue and often featuring different kinds of wordplay.

Examples of the traditional, dramatic story abound in both *The Ways of White Folks* and *Laughing To Keep From Crying*. They include, but are certainly not limited to, "Cora Unashamed," "Home," "Rejuvenation through Joy," "The Blues I'm Playing," and "Father and Son" (from *Ways*), and "Something in Common," "Who's Passing for Who?", and "Professor" (from *Laughing*). In such stories, what might be variously called the external action, the dramatic situation, or the fictional conflict, is clear and immediately recognizable. Indeed, in some stories such as "Who's Passing for Who?" the situational irony is so obvious it seems forced. By working in a mode with a clear beginning, middle, and end, and with a sharply defined conflict, Hughes employs a plot-driven form against which Chekhov, James, Hemingway, Joyce, and Mansfield—in the critical parlance—revolted.

Hughes's narrative counterrevolution in favor of plot did not spring from literary conservatism, however, nor from an antipathy to Joyce, Mansfield, or any of the writers who would later be termed modernists. Hughes's main link to the modernists after all, is D. H. Lawrence, himself an odd-person-out with regard to narrative style and structure. In part because he was inspired by Lawrence's direct, socially alert stories, Hughes started writing short fiction with social critique uppermost in mind. A lyrical, elliptical, subtle mode would not have served the purpose of presenting "the ways of white folks" and the collisions in society that racism caused. In other words, Hughes was often if not always drawn to the relatively uncomplicated narrative vehicle exemplified by Lawrence's fiction because it enabled him to dramatize racial friction. Ironically, what is so original about his short fiction, its economic and social critique of the racial "landscape," is exactly the element that drew him in many instances to a tried-and-true, conservative narrative mode. By contrast, Joyce, Mansfield, Hemingway, and Stein all seem nearly obsessed with the stylistic "surface" of their stories, even if these writers offer social critique of a different kind.

Style was not irrelevant to Hughes, certainly, but in comparison to the social urgency with which he wrote, it was not central either. Stories like "Cora Unashamed" have a style, to be sure, but they also clearly show that their author was not focused on prose stylishness in the same way Joyce, Mansfield, or Hemingway were. Moreover, stories such as "African Morning" and "Saratoga Rain" reveal that Hughes could write a more evocative kind of story when he was moved to do so. The presence of these stories in his body of work demonstrates the degree to which he deliberately chose to work in narrative modes not characterized by lyricism.

Ironically, one other mode that dominates Hughes's fiction is the sketch, which is in one way the opposite of the plot-driven, dramatic story. Hughes wrote in his journalistically-influenced, reportorial style most noticeably in *Laughing to Keep From Crying*: "Little Old Spy," "Pushcart Man," "Name in the Papers," and "Madame Shanghai" are good examples. In such stories, Hughes seems less politically urgent and more concerned with giving his readers a piece of "life-as-it-is-lived." And indeed, these stories seem to spring either from his travels ("Little Old Spy") or from his experience in Harlem ("Madame Shanghai"). Working in this mode seemed to let Hughes record or document the feel of a Harlem street or the atmosphere of Cuba.

It should be emphasized, as noted above, that with the anthropologist/writer Zora Neale Hurston, he shared a steadfast commitment to everyday African-American life as a source for art. Hurston and Hughes shared a fierce loyalty to folk art, whether it was southern black folktales, in Hurston's case, or the blues, in Hughes's. So while the sketch-stories are obviously the least dramatized, least "fictionalized," and perhaps least ambitious of his short stories, they still spring from the critical ethos expressed in "The Negro Artist and the Racial Mountain," in which he urged his fellow writers to make art out of their own experience, without apology. That is, just as Dickens recorded London in his sketches and Joyce recorded Dublin in the notebook-like *Stephen Hero*, Hughes sought to record the milieu he knew best. With Dickens and Joyce and Hurston, Hughes shared an ethnographic impulse. In the context of American literary history, Hughes's use of the sketch mode links him to local colorists of the nineteenth century, who also wrote out of an Anglo-American folk tradition. Just as importantly, the sketches would to some degree metamorphose into the streetwise Simple stories in the latter part of Hughes's career. In some way, that is, they may have prepared Hughes to write the Simple stories. Their informality, ironically, eventually led to the sharply defined, tight form of the Simple stories. In those numerous Jesse B. Simple narratives, we are treated to a short-story writer with a magnificent ear both for the "street speech" of Simple and the "colleged" speech of Boyd, and to a writer with a marvelous sense of comic timing, ironic undercutting, punning, and other techniques the spare structure masks. It is in these stories that Hughes defines and exploits to the fullest the talk-oriented mode of short fiction.

Because the Simple stories embody many of the critical tenets Hughes defined early in his career, it may be tempting to overlook how different they are from his other short fiction; but if only *The Ways of White Folks* and *Laughing to Keep From Crying* were examined, Hughes would not be judged a master of the dialogue-based short story. The Simple stories clearly allowed him to link the orality of his plays and poetry with the short-fiction genre, without abandoning other elements which had made his earlier stories successful: his political and social alertness; his eye for dramatic situations; his allegiance to everyday subjects; and his psychological acumen.

Certainly, Hughes's milieu, his preoccupations, were significantly different from those of Ernest Hemingway, but in the Simple stories, Hughes equaled the Hemingway of "Hills Like White Elephants" or "A Clean, Well-Lighted Place," in his capacity to base a narrative almost entirely on dialogue and make it succeed. The Simple stories bringing Hughes acclaim for their humor, accessibility, and topicality, also earn him a place among the best innovators of short fiction.

Epilogue

Hughes's Achievement in Short Fiction

Among the questions the previous chapters have tried implicitly to answer are these: what role did short fiction play in Hughes's career, and what did Hughes contribute to the history of short fiction? As a way of summing up a detailed discussion of the stories, perhaps now we can turn to some conclusive reflections on these key questions.

As much as any genre he attempted, short fiction seemed to give Hughes an artistic mode with which to take on issues of race and class in America and to dramatize the inequities, the exploitation, and the violence he experienced or witnessed. In many instances, the stories also allowed him to describe the particular psychosexual dimensions of race and class in America. As assertive and pointed as Hughes's poetry, essays, and plays can be, the most powerful social critique to be found in his writing may well reside in his short stories.

Short fiction also allowed him another avenue through which to express his affinity for common people. Indeed, the short stories seem to suggest that "uncommon" people were, in Hughes's mind, merely those who hubristically imagined themselves to be out of the ordinary. There is a marvelous and consistent ethnographic impulse in Hughes's fiction, a desire to provide a thick description of what he saw and heard. The Harlem character Jesse B. Simple is in many ways the apotheosis of this affinity for everyday concerns; his stories show how deftly Hughes could draw on folk elements, and how much power he could generate through a spare, highly conversational narrative form and a naive central character. In a lot of ways, short fiction was a mode well-suited to Hughes's particular gifts.

What Hughes contributed to the history of short fiction is first and foremost a bold, original African-American voice that could not be ignored, a voice which provided a model for later generations. When critics and literary historians assess African-American fiction, they tend to think of Claude McKay, Richard Wright, Ralph Ellison, James Baldwin, and, more recently, Toni Morrison and Alice Walker. These and other authors' achievements in the novel understandably sometimes divert attention from African-American short fiction in general and from

Hughes's short fiction in particular, but *in* the genre of short fiction, Hughes may well be the most influential African-American writer before 1950. He showed how adaptable the form was to social critique and to African-American literary traditions; he showed how writers could use the form simultaneously to appeal to a primarily black audience as well as "mainstream" white readers. In a variety of ways, he demonstrated that short fiction was a supple and open a form as verse had become after the advent of modernism.

Although Hughes's achievement in short fiction may be less monumental or mythic than that of Wright's, Ellison's, Baldwin's, Morrison's, or Walker's, it is no less crucial. Moreover, one can see clear traces of his influence in the short stories of recent African-American writers, including Alice Walker, whose oft-reprinted story, "Everyday Use," expresses an ethos similar to Hughes's, Ernest Gaines, J. California Cooper, Rita Dove, and Randall Kenan, to name but a few.

Further, as this study has previously discussed, Hughes defined a kind of short fiction that was markedly different from modernist models, and for this reason, too, his achievement is more than merely noteworthy. As mentioned earlier, his chief connection to modernism is D. H. Lawrence, another anomalous modernist; otherwise, Hughes's stories tend to be more direct and plot-oriented, less lyrical and oblique than the fiction of Joyce, Hemingway, and Mansfield, for example. As discussed earlier Hughes also draws considerably on an African-American tradition of ironic discourse now known as "Signifying."

Paradoxical Hughes

In general, studying Hughes's short fiction brings into sharper relief the key paradoxes inherent in his art and career. For Hughes is an unusual combination of the proletarian and the cosmopolite, the folk artist and the renaissance man, the loner and the voice of the people, the nationalist and the internationalist. Let's briefly take a closer look at these unusual, sometimes paradoxical, combinations of impulses, traits, and characteristics, beginning with Hughes as "proletarian cosmopolite."

Very few short story writers of his generation revealed as much sympathy for and unsentimental understanding of the working class as Hughes did. From his first collection through the Simple stories, his interest in the economically-marginalized and his awareness of class issues remained authentic and steady. It is ironic that the *Partisan Review*, in one of the few expressly unfavorable reviews of *The Ways of*

White Folks, dismissed the book for containing "very little that is revolutionary" and for not being sufficiently political.[26] Certainly, Hughes was not political in any narrow, programmatic way, nor was he a well-defined "leftist" in the way the *Partisan Review* might have defined the term, but his assessments of race and class in America were sophisticated and sharp, especially in *The Ways of White Folks*. Nor did his affinity for the working class end with that important collection of stories.

However, his own instincts were surprisingly cosmopolitan for a writer with such close ties to the working class and such an affinity for regional sensibilities; having traveled incessantly until his health broke down, he weaves that peripatetic experience almost effortlessly into his short fiction. It is difficult to think of other American writers who have set their stories in so many cities, regions, and continents: Harlem, New York City, Los Angeles, Reno, the Midwest, the South, the West, Europe, Africa, Asia, the Carribean.

Similarly, it is rare to find a writer so attuned to folk traditions such as jazz, "the dozens," the blues, and evangelical discourse. Hughes enjoyed major achievements in poetry, drama, autobiography, fiction, and journalism, and with "The Negro Artist and the Racial Mountain," he helped forge an ethos that would lead to the Black Aesthetic. In his short fiction, this apparent contrast of folk artist/renaissance writer plays out in interesting ways. The material to which Hughes is drawn is often folk-oriented or at least working-class. Hughes's renaissance temperament reveals itself in his experiments with so many techniques and points of view, with different kinds of dramatic, comic, and sketch or "reportage" forms, and with many levels of literary diction. This temperament is also reflected in the many different kinds of publications to which Hughes contributed stories, from *The New Yorker* to the *Brooklyn Daily Eagle* to the *Chicago Defender*.

The problems Hughes had with his native country were numerous and real, and they informed much of his writing; he was a fair, generous, but unrelenting critic of American society. Nonetheless, he pushed himself and urged fellow black writers to make art out of their American experience. While he understood the forces which drove writers to become expatriates, he himself resisted the option of leaving for good. As noted above, the settings of his stories are extraordinarily far-flung, but there is also a sense in which Harlem provides a gravitational center to his fiction, creating a place of return.

What may be even more paradoxical or at least more ironic about Hughes's "Americanness" is that his writing became an inspiration for the pan-national literary/cultural movement known as "Negritude." Such international influence attests to the fact that Hughes could, in his short fiction particularly, make use of his American experience without ignoring or negating his African heritage or without seeming too regional, local, or provincial. Indeed, Hughes articulated the ways in which American history, society, and culture had changed owing to the presence of African Americans.

A study of his short fiction, at any rate, is not only valuable in its own right, but also offers a revealing cross section of the conflicting impulses, uncommon paradoxes, and many loyalties of Langston Hughes, who remains one of America's most versatile, complicated, and moral writers.

Notes To Part 1

1. David Nifong, "Narrative Technique and Theory in *The Ways of White Folks,*" *Black American Literature Forum* 15 (Fall 1981): 96.

2. James Emanuel, "'Bodies in the Moonlight,': A Critical Analysis," in *Critical Essays On Langston Hughes*, ed. Edward J. Mullen (Boston: G.K. Hall, 1986), 178.

3. Arnold Rampersad, *The Life of Langston Hughes, Volume I: 1902–1941* (New York: Oxford University Press, 1986), 269. This volume hereafter cited in the text as Rampersad, I.

4. Henry Louis Gates, Jr., *The Signifying Monkey: A Theory of African-American Literary Criticism* (New York: Oxford University Press, 1988), 100–01.

5. Houston A. Baker, Jr., *Blues, Ideology, and Afro-American Literature: A Vernacular Theory* (Chicago: University of Chicago Press, 1984), 96–97.

6. Langston Hughes, *The Ways of White Folks* (New York: Knopf, 1934), 3; hereafter cited in the text as *Ways*.

7. Berndt Ostendorf, *Black Literature In White America* (Sussex: The Harvester Press, 1982), 122.

8. R. Baxter Miller, *The Art and Imagination of Langston Hughes* (Lexington: University Press of Kentucky, 1989), 104; hereafter cited in the text as Miller.

9. *Laughing To Keep From Crying* (New York: Henry Holt, 1952), 2; hereafter cited in the text as *Laughing*.

10. Arnold Rampersad, *The Life of Langston Hughes, Vol. 2: 1941–1967* (New York: Oxford University Press, 1988), 61–67; this volume hereafter cited in the text as Rampersad, 2.

11. *The Big Sea* (New York: Knopf, 1940) and *I Wonder As I Wander: An Autobiographical Journey* (New York: Hill and Wang, 1956).

12. *The Best of Simple* (New York: Hill and Wang, 1961), vii; hereafter cited in the text as Foreword.

13. "Feet Live Their Own Life," *The Best of Simple* (New York: Hill and Wang, 1961), 1.

14. "Summer Ain't Simple" and "Jealousy," *Simple Speaks His Mind* (New York: Simon and Schuster, 1950), 50–55, 79–82.

15. "Jazz, Jive, and Jam," *The Best of Simple* (New York: Hill and Wang, 1961), 243.

16. "The Blues," *Simple's Uncle Sam* (New York: Aeonian Press, 1965), 17–19; hereafter cited in the text as "The Blues."

17. "Adventure," *Simple's Uncle Sam* (New York: Aeonian Press, 1965), 65; hereafter cited in the text as "Adventure."

18. "Duty Is Not Snooty," *The Best of Simple* (New York: Hill and Wang, 1961), 196–98; hereafter cited in the text as "Duty."

19. "Seven Rings," *The Best of Simple* (New York: Hill and Wang, 1961), 94.

20. "A Toast to Harlem," *The Best of Simple* (New York: Hill and Wang: 1961), 20.

21. *Simple's Uncle Sam* (New York: Aeonian Press, 1965), 157.

22. Eugenia Collier, "A Pain In His Soul: Simple As Epic Hero," in *Langston Hughes: Black Genius: A Critical Evaluation*, ed. Therman B. O'Daniel (New York: William Morrow, 1971), 127.

23. James Emanuel, "The Short Fiction of Langston Hughes," in *Langston Hughes: Black Genius: a Critical Evaluation*, ed. Therman B. O'Daniel (New York: William Morrow, 1971), 156.

24. Blyden Jackson, "A Word About Simple," in *Langston Hughes: Black Genius: A Critical Evaluation*, ed. Therman B. O'Daniel (New York: William Morrow, 1971), 113.

25. *Something In Common and Other Stories* (New York: Hill and Wang, 1963); hereafter cited in the text as *Something In Common*.

26. Leon Dennen, "Negroes and Whites," *Partisan Review*, (November-December 1934):50. See also John E. Bassett, *Harlem in Review* (London and Toronto: Associated Universities Press, 1992), 29–30.

Part 2

THE WRITER

Introduction

While the purpose of Part 1 was to provide a thorough critical analysis of Hughes's short fiction, the purpose of this section is to hear from Hughes himself, at least insofar as he expressed himself in essays, speeches, and autobiographical writing.

Consequently, virtually no critical commentary accompanies the following excerpts. Because of its indisputable uniqueness as a document of Hughes's aesthetic ideas, the essay "The Negro Artist and the Racial Mountain" is the obvious source with which to begin the series of excerpts. For the same reason, selections from this essay demand a slightly more detailed introduction.

Otherwise, the minimal introductory material preceding subsequent excerpts is intended only to provide the simplest biographical or chronological framework, to tell where Hughes was living at the time the material was written, or to provide a few basic details about the publishing history of a piece.

"The Negro Artist and the Racial Mountain" appeared in *The Nation* in 1926. Hughes wrote the piece at the invitation of *The Nation*'s managing editor, Freda Kirchwey, who had sent him the proofs of George Schuyler's essay "The Negro-Art Hokum." Hughes biographer Arnold Rampersad has called the response to Schuyler "the finest essay of Hughes's life."[1]

Although the specific milieu of the essay was the Harlem Renaissance, and although the immediate context was a debate about what attitudes lay behind the current popularity of "Negro art," the essay reaches well beyond its time and essentially comprises a foundation for "the Black Aesthetic" that would develop decades later. It also shows that for African-American writers of Hughes's generation, literary aesthetics were necessarily enmeshed with politics because they were inevitably connected with race and class.

Furthermore, as noted above, the essay provides us with the clearest statement of the literary and political ideas that inform virtually every one of Hughes's short stories. And although Hughes wrote the essay

when he was twenty-four, he remained loyal to its main ideas until his
death, so it amounts to an apologia for his entire career:

> Certainly there is, for the American Negro artist who can escape the
> restrictions the more advanced among his own group would put upon
> him, a great field of unused material ready for his art. Without going
> outside his race, and even among the better classes with their "white"
> culture and conscious American manners, but still Negro enough to
> be different, there is sufficient matter to furnish a black artist with a
> lifetime of creative work. And when he chooses to touch on relations
> between Negroes and whites in this country with their innumerable
> overtones and undertones, surely, and especially for literature and the
> drama, there is an inexhaustible supply of themes at hand. To these
> the Negro artist can give his racial individuality, his heritage of rhythm
> and warmth, and his incongruous humor that so often, as in the Blues,
> becomes ironic laughter mixed with tears.[2]

Later in the essay, Hughes writes: "The Negro artist works against an
undertow of sharp criticism and misunderstanding from his own group
and unintentional bribes from the whites. 'Oh, be respectable, write
about nice people, show how good we are,' says the Negroes. 'Be
stereotyped, don't go too far, don't shatter our illusions about you, don't
amuse us too seriously. We will pay you,' say the whites" ("The Negro
Artist," 693).

Some thirty years after his crucial essay appeared, Hughes spoke
before the national assembly of authors and dramatists, as part of a
symposium on "The Writer's Position In America" (Alvin Theatre, New
York City, 7 May 1957). One note of clarification is in order: Hughes gave
the speech during the Jesse B. Simple part of his career; however, the
one short story to which Hughes refers specifically is probably "Home,"
the story about lynching from *The Ways of White Folks*:

> I once sent one of my best known short stories, before it came out in
> book form, to one of our oldest and foremost American magazines.
> The story was about racial violence in the South. It came back to me
> with a very brief little note saying the editor did not believe his
> readers wished to read about such things. Another story of mine which
> did not concern race problems at all came back to me from one of our
> best known editors of anthologies of fiction with a letter praising the
> story but saying he, the editor, could not tell if the characters were
> white or colored. Would I make them definitely Negro? Just a plain

story about human beings from me was not up his alley, it seems. So before the word man I simply inserted black, and before the girl's name, the words brown skin—and the story was accepted. Only a mild form of racial bias.[3]

Later in the speech, he addresses the enormous appeal an expatriate experience has for African-American writers. The passage deserves to be included here because it implicitly describes the ambivalence Hughes might have felt about staying in Harlem during the difficult 1950s:

> We have in America today about a dozen top flight, frequently published and really good Negro writers. Do you not think it strange that of that dozen, at least half of them live abroad, far away from their people, their problems, and the sources of their material: Richard Wright—"Native Son" in Paris; Chester Himes—"The Primitives" in Paris; James Baldwin—"Giovanni's Room" in Paris; William Denby—"Beetle Creek" in Rome; Ralph Ellison—"Invisible Man" in Rome; Frank Yerby—of the dozen best sellers, in South France; and Willard Motley—"Knock On Any Door" in Mexico. Why: Because the stones thrown at Autherine Lucy at the University of Alabama are thrown at them, too. Because the shadow of Montgomery and the bombs under Rev. King's house, shadow them and shatter them, too. Because the body of little Emmett Till drowned in a Mississippi river and no one brought to justice, haunts them, too. One of the writers I've mentioned, when last I saw him before he went abroad, said to me, "I don't want my children to grow up in the shadow of Jim Crow." (Reader, 484)

Although Hughes wrote two autobiographies, neither one contains the font of information about writing in general or his short stories in particular that one might expect. (Hughes tended to be a terse, matter-of-fact writer in his autobiographies, just as he tended to be reticent in his everyday life.) Nonetheless, some excerpts shed light on important issues related to his short stories.

For example, "When the Negro Was in Vogue," a chapter from *The Big Sea* (Hughes's first autobiography), provides a context for the stories in *The Ways of White Folks* that deal with the "exoticism" of "Negro art":

> White people began to come to Harlem in droves. For several years they packed the expensive Cotton Club on Lenox Avenue. But I was never there, because the Cotton Club was a Jim Crow club for gangsters and monied whites. They were not cordial to Negro patron-

age, unless you were a celebrity like Bojangles. So Harlem Negroes did not like the Cotton Club and never appreciated its Jim Crow policy in the very heart of their dark community. Nor did ordinary Negroes like the growing influx of whites toward Harlem after sundown, flooding the little cabarets and bars where formerly only colored people laughed and sang, and where now the strangers were given the best ringside tables to sit and stare at the Negro customers— like amusing animals in a zoo.[4]

In the chapter "Harlem Literati," Hughes describes the "scene" of the Harlem Renaissance, concentrating on such figures as Wallace Thurman, who helped him publish his early writing, and Zora Neale Hurston, with whom he shared an intense interest in African-American folk traditions:

> About the future of Negro literature, Thurman was very pessimistic. He thought the Negro vogue had made us all too conscious of ourselves, had flattered and spoiled us, and had provided too many easy opportunities for some of us to drink gin and more gin, on which he thought we would always be drunk. With his bitter sense of humor, he called the Harlem literati, the "niggerati." Of this "niggerati," Zora Neale Hurston was certainly the most amusing. Only to reach a wider audience, need she ever write books—because she is a perfect book of entertainment in herself. . . . Almost nobody else could stop the average Harlemite on Lenox Avenue and measure his head with a strange-looking, anthropological device and not get bawled out for the attempt, except Zora, who used to stop anyone whose head looked interesting, and measure it. (*The Big Sea*, 233–38)

One of the last chapters ("Literary Quarrel") gives Hughes's version of his feud with Hurston over the authorship of the play *Mule Bone*:

> On the evening I arrived in Cleveland [in January 1931], the Gilpin Players, America's oldest Negro theatre group, were performing a new play and I went to see it, thinking it might ease my mind. After the performance, I was talking with the director, Rowena Jelliffe, and she told me that she had just received an excellent Negro folk comedy by a talented young woman named Zora Hurston. I expressed interest, so she went on to tell me that it was about a quarrel between two rival church factions in the deep South, that it was a very amusing play, and that it was called *Mule Bone*. She said it had just been turned down by

the Theatre Guild in New York, but that an agent had sent a rough draft to her with permission to try it out in Cleveland.

From the description and title, I knew it was the same play Zora Hurston and I had worked on together. But it was not finished and it did not seem to me it should be produced in that form. (*The Big Sea*, 331–32)

At this point, the feud erupted, and the play was never produced. Hughes writes,

> That evening [several days later] my fraternity brothers were giving a dance in my honor [in Cleveland]. I had informed them three days before that the doctor had forbidden me to leave my bed [because of complications arising from a tonsilectomy] and that I could not come to any dance. But since it was all arranged, they went ahead with it just the same. In my honor, Miss Hurston, being a visiting celebrity, was invited to the party, since the brothers knew nothing of our literary quarrel. With a local young man, she went to the ball and told everyone how awful I was. Then she drove back to New York. As soon as I recovered my voice, I called up the local young man to tell him I meant to beat the hell out of him.
>
> I never heard from Miss Hurston again. Unfortunately, our art was broken, and that was the end of what would have been a good play had it ever been finished—the first real Negro folk comedy—*Mule Bone*. (*The Big Sea*, 333–34)

The feud was one of the most excruciating ironies to emerge from the Harlem Renaissance, for their allegiance to folk traditions made Hughes and Hurston the most similar—and eventually the most influential—writers of the Renaissance.

It should be stressed that Hughes's version of the feud is only his version. (An exhaustive study of the disagreement—including letters between Hughes, Hurston, and other principals—accompanies a recent publication of *Mule Bone*, edited by George Houston Bass and Henry Louis Gates, Jr.)[5]

In Hughes's second autobiography, *I Wonder As I Wander* (1956), appears his most direct explanation of how he came to write the stories in *The Ways of White Folks* and of D. H. Lawrence's influence on those stories. The tale begins in Russia, where Hughes had gone in 1932 to work on an ill-fated film project. He writes:

> The circumstances of my beginning to write [short stories] were curious. Shortly after I moved into the New Moscow Hotel, I met

there Marie Seaton from London. . . . [She] had with her a paper-bound copy of D. H. Lawrence's short stories, The Lovely Lady, which she lent me. I had never read anything of Lawrence's before, and was particularly taken with the title story, and with "The Rocking Horse Winner." Both tales made my hair stand on end. . . . A night or two after I had read the Lawrence stories, I sat down to write an Izvestia article on Tashkent when, instead, I began to write a short story. I had been saying to myself all day, "If D.H. Lawrence can write such psychologically powerful accounts of folks in England, that send shiver up and down my spine, maybe I could write stories like his about folks in America. I wonder."[6]

A bit later in the same chapter, Hughes describes the origins of the story "Cora Unashamed":

> I began to turn over in my mind a story that a young lawyer in California, Loren Miller, had told me. He said that in one of the small towns in Kansas where he had lived during his childhood, there had been a very pretty colored girl who, as she grew up, attracted the amorous eye of the town's only Negro doctor, the town's only Negro undertaker, and the town's Negro ministers. All three of these men enjoyed her favors. The girl became pregnant. But by whom? . . . When I sat down at my well-traveled typewriter and began to write my first short story, "Cora Unashamed," the material of the factual narrative I'd heard from Loren Miller changed into fiction. The Negro girl became a white girl of middle-class family, whose parents did not want her to fall in love with an immigrant Greek boy whose father ran an ice-cream stand. (*I Wonder*, 214)

The following passage, taken from an essay Hughes wrote in the mid-1950s, discusses Hughes's own view of how jazz shaped his ideas about literature:

> Jazz seeps into words—spelled out words. Nelson Algren is influenced by jazz. Ralph Ellison is, too. Sartre, too. Jacques Prevert. Most of the best writers today are. Look at the end of The Ballad of the Sad Cafe. Me as the public, my dot in the middle—it was fifty years ago, the first time I heard the Blues on Independence Avenue in Kansas City. Then State Street in Chicago. Then Harlem in the twenties with J. P. and J. C. Johnson and Fats and Willie the Lion and Nappy playing piano—with the Blues running all up and down the keyboard through the ragtime and the jazz. (*Reader*, 493)

As deeply as Hughes sank roots in Harlem, he remained an inveterate traveler, and in 1933 he journeyed to and lived on the West Coast, first in San Francisco, then in Carmel, with a trip to Reno thrown in. During this time, he wrote many stories and met several writers, artists, musicians, and actors: "The prelude to work at Hyde Street [in San Francisco] was delightful for . . . fascinating guests were coming and going daily: Judith Anderson, Duke Ellington, Marie Welch, Roland Hayes, Jose Iturbi, the young William Saroyan, Kenneth Spencer, Krishnamurti, Elsie Arden, Dwight Fiske, Marian Anderson, bearded old Colonel Wood and soft-spoken Sara Bard Field, and the Irish Hebrew, Albert Bender" (*I Wonder*, 282).

After leaving San Francisco to spend time in Carmel, where he got to know writers Robinson Jeffers and Lincoln Steffens, Hughes wrote numerous stories:

> My stories written at Carmel all dealt with some nuance of the race problem. Most of them had their roots in actual situations which I had heard about or in which I had been myself involved. But none of them were literal transcriptions of actual happenings. All of the stories I wrote at Carmel were sold to magazines, and one of them, "A Good Job Gone," concerning miscegenation, created a furor in *Esquire*, hundreds of letters pouring in to the editor, some extremely heated. Fourteen of the stories appeared in my Knopf book, *The Ways of White Folk*. Others were published in a later collection, *Laughing To Keep From Crying*. . . . At Carmel I worked ten or twelve hours a day, and turned out at least one story or completed article every week, sometimes more. (*I Wonder*, 285)

According to Hughes, the trip to Reno provided the germ for at least two other stories.

> Ernestine Black, a friend of Noel Sullivan's, had invited a group of folks for a late-summer weekend at her cabin on Lake Taho [*sic*] in the High Sierras where pallets were spread on sleeping verandas under the stars. I had always wanted to see Reno so, being near the California-Nevada border, I decided to go there. In Reno I stayed about a month and gathered the material for a story called "Slice Him Down" published in *Esquire*. Also in Reno the germ of the idea for one of my best stories, "On the Road," came to me. The background for both stories was the American depression, then in full sway.
> Reno was a convenient stopping-off place for penniless travelers

riding the rods between the East and West. Just outside the town there was a large hobo jungle. Many hungry Negroes from the East came through Reno in freight cars, heading for San Francisco where they thought times might be better. (*I Wonder*, 286)

And so the material from *I Wonder As I Wander* that refers to Hughes's West-Coast travels sheds light not just Hughes the writer but on Hughes the person: part loner and part extrovert. In fact, Hughes's friend, Arna Bontemps, once characterized him as being "trapped between two powerful impulses—his passionate love of people and his compelling need for isolation" (*Rampersad*, 1:340).

Later in the 1930s, Hughes was to travel to Spain to write about politics of a different sort, the Spanish revolution. In *I Wonder As I Wander* he describes his state of mind just before his departure and his reaction to the success of prizefighter Joe Louis:

> When I got on the boat to go to Europe, in the spring of 1937 to cover the Spanish Civil War, I could hardly speak above a whisper. The night before I left Cleveland, Joe Louis had become a heavy-weight champion of the world, so I had ridden around for hours in a car full of folks shouting and yelling after the news of Braddock's defeat came over the radio. I do not believe Negro America has ever before or since had a national hero like Joe Louis. As he went up the ladder toward the championship, and after he became champion, winning fight after fight, Louis became a kind of symbol of all that Negroes had always dreamed of in American life. Then, as the Nazi threat in Europe became more and more pronounced, he became for the Negro people through the world a champion of racial decency and achieve-ment, the one who could and was giving a lie to the Hitler blood theory of white supremacy—which our own American Red Cross was later to adopt to the hurt and horror of black Americans.
>
> Each time Joe Louis won a fight in those depression years, even before he became champion, thousands of colored Americans on relief or W.P.A., and poor, would throng out into the streets all across the land to march and cheer and yell and cry because of Joe's one-man triumphs. (*I Wonder*, 314–15)

While he was in Spain, Hughes encountered numerous writers, from Pablo Neruda to Ernest Hemingway:

> Among the non-English speaking writers I encountered were André Malraux, Juan de la Cabada and Audres Iduarte whom I had

known in Mexico; Pablo Neruda, Alfred Kantorowicz, Ludwig Renn, Ernst Toller, Gustav Regler, Ilya Ehrenburg, Michael Koltsov, Jef Lat, and a number of others from Middle Europe and Scandinavia whose names I can't remember now. Certainly the most celebrated American in Spain was Ernest Hemingway. I found him a big likeable fellow whom the men in the Brigades adored. He spent a great deal of time with them in their encampments. Hemingway himself had been under fire more than once, and he lived in one of the most vulnerable buildings of Madrid, the Hotel Florida. I ran into him and the golden-haired Martha Gellhorn from time to time, and spent a whole day with Hemingway the late summer at the Brigade Auto Park on the edge of the city where my friends, Rucker and Battle, were stationed. I don't remember now what we talked about, nothing very profound, I'm sure, and there was a lot of kidding as we shared the meal with the men. (*I Wonder*, 364).

About six years after traveling to Spain, Hughes wrote a brief essay called "My America." "I am an American," he writes midway through the essay—"but I am a colored American." He continues,

Jim Crowism varies in degree from North to South, from the mixed schools and free franchise of Michigan to the tumbledown colored schools and open terror at the polls of Georgia and Mississippi. All over America, however, against the Negro there has been a economic color line of such severity that since the Civil War we have been kept most effectively, as a racial group, in the lowest economic brackets. Statistics are not needed to prove this. Simply look around you on the Main Street of any American town or city. There are no colored clerks in any of the stores—although colored people spend their money there. There are practically never any colored street-car conductors or bus drivers—although these public carriers run over streets for which we pay taxes. There are no colored girls at the switchboards of the telephone company—but millions of Negroes have phone and pay their bills. . . . Yet America is a land where, in spite of its defects, I can write this article. Here the voice of democracy is still heard—Roosevelt, Wallace, Wilkie, Agar, Pearl Buck, Paul Robeson. America is a land where the poll tax still holds in the South but opposition to the poll tax grows daily. . . . America is a land where the best of all democracies has been achieved for some people—but in Georgia, Roland Hayes, world-famous singer, is beaten for being colored and nobody is jailed—nor can Mr. Hayes vote in the State where he was born. Yet America is a country where Roland Hayes can come from a log cabin to wealth and fame—in spite of the segment that still wishes to maltreat him physically and spiritually, famous though he is. (*Reader*, 500–501)

Toward the end of his life, Hughes reflected on his preoccupation with politics and matters of race and class, and Part 2 will conclude with an excerpt from that reflection:

> Politics in any country in the world is dangerous. For the poet, politics in any country in the world had better be disguised as poetry. . . . Politics can be the graveyard of the poet. And only poetry can be his resurrection. What is poetry? It is the human soul entire, squeezed like as lemon or a lime, drop by drop, into atomic words. The ethnic language does not matter. Ask Aimé Césaire. He knows. Perhaps not consciously—but in the soul of his writing, he knows. The Negritudinous Senghor, the Caribbeanesque Guillen, the American me, are regional poets of genuine realities and authentic values. Cesaire . . . takes all that we have, Senghor, Guillen, and Hughes, and flings it at the moon, to make of it a space-ship of the dreams of all the dreamers in the world. As a footnote I must add that, concerning Cesaire, all I have said I deeply feel is for me true. Concerning politics, nothing I have said is true. A poet is a human being. Each human being must live within his time, with and for his people, with within the boundaries of his country. Therefore, how can a poet keep out of politics? Hang yourself, poet, in your own words. Otherwise, you are dead. (*Rampersad*, 2:295)

As we move on to Part 3, "The Critics," we might pause for a moment to observe that the late, unpublished piece of exploratory writing quoted above shows how self-conflicted Hughes was concerning the connection between writing and politics. The piece reveals a kind of weariness and cynicism about politics, but then, toward the end, it reaffirms Hughes's belief that writing is grounded in history and social conflict. Further, the phrase "genuine realities and authentic values" may capture the quintessential Hughes and certainly describes the ethos of his short fiction.

Notes to Part 2

1. Arnold Rampersad, *The Life of Langston Hughes* (New York: Oxford University Press, 1986), 1:130; hereafter cited as Rampersad.

2. "The Negro Artist and the Racial Mountain," *Nation* 23 June 1926: 692; hereafter edited in the text.

3. "A Speech at the National Assembly of Authors and Dramatists: The Negro Writer's Position in America," in *The Langston Hughes Reader* (New York: Braziller, 1958), 483; hereafter cited in the text as *Reader*.

4. *The Big Sea* (New York: Knopf, 1940), 224–25; hereafter cited in the text.

5. Written with Zora Neale Hurston, *Mule Bone: A Comedy of Negro Life*, ed. George Houston Bass and Henry Louis Gates, Jr. (New York: Harper Perennial, 1991).

6. *I Wonder As I Wander* (New York: Hill and Wang, 1956), 213; hereafter cited in the text as *I Wonder*.

Part 3

THE CRITICS

Introduction

Certainly, there is no severe shortage of criticism and scholarship on Langston Hughes and his work, much of it concerning the poetry, his influential life, his connection with a momentous cultural movement (the Harlem Renaissance), and his prefiguration of the Black Aesthetic movement of the 1960s. In part because Hughes was "all over the map"—working in so many genres, producing so much material—the critical work about him springs from a variety of critical and theoretical perspectives.

Consequently, assessing criticism of his work and evaluations of his achievement is more complicated than it may be in the case of Katherine Anne Porter, Frank O'Connor, Katherine Mansfield, and other writers who worked with short fiction almost exclusively. Further, Hughes embarked on short fiction in mid-career; he had written a few stories as a young man, but he did not turn to the form with determination and purpose until he was in his thirties. As a result, reviews and even some later critical appraisals of the short fiction are tinged with well-established ideas about him, about his aesthetic ideas, and about his already established place in the American literary scene. For by 1934, when his first book of stories appeared, he had already been on the scene as poet, journalist, playwright, and essayist.

Therefore, chiefly because the Hughes criticism is so abundant, varied, and complicated, I have chosen to present many excerpts from articles and books, as opposed to presenting a few complete articles.

Before we turn to excerpts from Hughes's critics, Sherwood Anderson's memorable review of *The Ways of White Folks* in *The Nation* requires a moment of special scrutiny because it provides a natural bridge between the first two parts of this study and this concluding section.[1]

In the review, Anderson is deeply troubled by the pointed critique of white racism. Further, he perceives the harsh verbal and situational ironies in the stories as a form of unfair punishment; he sees the harshness as his (and other white readers') having to pay for the sins of slavery. Hence the title of the review, "Paying For Old Sins." Anderson clearly feels as if he and other white readers are victims of a verbal attack.

Anderson goes so far as to suggest a divided audience for the stories: "Mr. Hughes, my hat off to you in relation to your own race, but not to mine" (Anderson, 65). The purpose of this sentence is clear: Anderson suggests the stories will succeed for black Americans but not for whites; but the rhetorical stance of the sentence is perhaps more noteworthy than the purpose, for Anderson turns, as it were, from the reader of the review to speak directly (if figuratively) to "Mr. Hughes." In a sense, he lectures Langston Hughes briefly but sternly, even as he pretends to doff his hat. The posture of the sentence is defensive, as is the formal "Mr. Hughes." The suggestion of a black audience and a white one is divisive, and, ironically, it recapitulates some of the very "ways of white folks" that Hughes's stories critique.

The Anderson review is fascinating in other ways as well. It represents one renowned writer's assessment of another's work, for one thing. For another, it shows how deeply *The Ways of White Folks* had struck a nerve and engendered defensiveness with its determined, unabashed portrayal of racial friction.

Moreover, Anderson's review shows the degree to which Hughes's preference for a direct style—influenced by D. H. Lawrence—"collided" with the more distanced, polished modernist style. At the end of the review, Anderson declaims, "There are always too many story tellers using their talents to get even with life. There is a plane to be got on—the impersonal" (Anderson, 66). In Anderson's view of the short story, Hughes had gone out of bounds by being too political, too direct, too transparently opinionated. To put the matter in the terms used by Henry James, a chief proponent of an "impersonal" style, Hughes had "told, not shown." Further, Anderson perceives a single literary model—he calls it a "plane"—to be emulated, which is "the impersonal."

Whether one sides with Hughes or Anderson on the issue of the "impersonal style" matters less than recognizing Anderson's response to Hughes as an important moment in the history of American short fiction, and as a doorway to subsequent criticism represented by the following selections.

Alain Locke

These fourteen short stories of Negro-white contacts told from the unusual angle of the Negro point of view are challenging to all who would understand the later phases of the race question as it takes on the new complications of contemporary social turmoil and class struggle. Their sociological significance is as important as their literary value, perhaps more so, because although written with some personal reaction of disillusionment and despair, they reflect the growing resentment and desperation which is on the increase in the Negro world today. Though harped upon almost to the extent of a formula, there is an important warning in what has been called "the sullen, straight, bitter realism" of this book. It has a reportorial courage and presents new angles, but it offers no solutions, doctors no situations and points no morals.

From an untitled review of *The Ways of White Folks*, *Survey Graphic* 23 (November 1934): 565.

Arna Bontemps

Few people have enjoyed being Negro as much as Langston Hughes. Despite the bitterness with which he has occasionally indicated those who mistreat him because of his color (and in this collection of sketches and stories he certainly does not let up), there has never been any question in this reader's mind about his basic attitude. He would not have missed the experience of being what he is for the world. . . . Langston Hughes has practised the craft of the short story no more than he has practised the forms of poetry. His is a spontaneous art which stands or falls by the sureness of his intuition, his mother wit. His stories, like his poems, are for readers who will judge them with their hearts as well as their heads. By that standard he has always measured well. He still does.

From "Black and Bubbling," a review of *Laughing to Keep From Crying, Saturday Review of Literature* 35 (5 April 1952): 17.

Carl Van Vechten

It is not generally known as it should be that Langston Hughes laughs with, cries with, and speaks for the Negro (in all classes) more understandingly, perhaps, than any other writer. Harlem is his own habitat, his workshop and his playground, his forte and his dish of tea. He is so completely at home when he writes about Harlem that he can afford to be both careless and sloppy. In his Simple books he is seldom either, and *Simple Takes A Wife* is a superior achievement to the first of the series, *Simple Speaks His Mind*. The new book is more of a piece, the material is more carefully and competently arranged, more unexpectedly presented, it is more brilliant, more skillfully written, funnier, and perhaps just a shade more tragic than its predecessor.

From "In the Heart of Harlem," a review of *Simple Takes A Wife*, *New York Times*, 31 May 1953, 5.

Luther Jackson

In a foreword to this book of sketches on the life and times of Harlem's Jesse B. Semple, better known as Simple, the author suggests that a humorous Negro monthly magazine would be a welcome addition to American life. Expanding this idea, Hughes lists 16 potential contributors—including cartoonists, journalists, novelists and comedians, ranging from Jackie Mabley to George S. Schuyler.

This reviewer would never sell a Hughes' idea short, for his brainchildren have enjoyed some 30 years of artistic success. But with Simple, Hughes has struck commercial gold. He has exploited the vein to the extent of three books and a Broadway theatrical production, all adapted from newspaper columns from the *Chicago Defender*.

Hughes' and Simple's successes are well deserved, for in Jesse B. the author has created a tribute to the dignity of a common man who happens to be a Negro. This is no mean trick. In hands less skilled than Hughes', portrayals of some Negroes—"colleged" as well as "uncolleged"—are apt to wind up in racial embarrassment.

From an untitled review of *Simple Stakes A Claim*, *Crisis* 64 (May 1957): 576–77.

Melvin Tolson

Countee Cullen and Langston Hughes represent the antipodes of the Harlem Renaissance. The former is a classicist and conservative; the latter, an experimentalist and radical. . . . Hughes, the rebel, is a bold enemy of economic and racial injustice and often dipped his pen in the acid of satire.

From "Langston Hughes," *Critical Essays on Langston Hughes*, ed. Edward J. Mullen (Boston: G.K. Hall, 1986), 120–24. This excerpt is from 120 and 124.

Arnold Rampersad

With this collection [*The Ways of White Folks*], Hughes repeated in the short story the feat he had already accomplished both in poetry and in the novel; he set a new standard of excellence for black writers. Compared to [Hughes's novel] *Not Without Laughter*, *The Ways of White Folks* is far more adult and neurotic, more militant and defensive, and thus more modern and accurate as a description of the Afro-American temper as it was emerging.

From *The Life of Langston Hughes* (New York: Oxford University Press, 1986), 1:290.

Onwuchekwa Jemie

Hughes's confidence in blackness is a major part of his legacy, for the questions he had to answer have had to be answered over again by subsequent generations of black artists. Black culture is still embattled; and Hughes provides a model for answering questions and making the choices. . . . His central concern is the concern of the Afro-American people, namely, their struggle for freedom. His is, from first to last, a socially committed literature, utilizing, for a brief period of time at least, a Marxist ideological framework.

From "Hughes's Black Aesthetic," *Critical Essays on Langston Hughes*, ed. Edward J. Mullen (Boston: G.K. Hall, 1986), 95–119. This excerpt is taken from 114–15.

R. Baxter Miller

While the presence of Judaeo-Christian redemption in "Berry" alters potential tragedy into comedy, "Father and Son" (1934)—possibly Hughes's best-crafted fiction—more closely follows the conventions of tragedy. . . . Although the plot lines are too sentimental and awkward, they do help to reveal the connection between the psychology of power and the relationship of one culture's rise and another's fall. Both Bert [the son] and Norwood [the father] function within the same myth as a big rise on the horizon but seems quite fallen in the end—not the physical structure but the [cultural] premise upon which it stands. . . . The white assumes a linear movement through Western time from the past through the present to the future. He assumes an advance into tragic death. But Simple draws upon African roots in which past, present, and future occupy different levels of hierarchical existence within one continuous time.

From *The Art and Imagination of Langston Hughes* (Lexington: University Press of Kentucky, 1989), 110.

Arthur P. Davis

The outstanding contribution . . . which Hughes has made in his delineation of the tragic mulatto, it seems to me, is to point out that at bottom the problem of mixed-blood is basically a personal problem. Hughes reduces the tragic mulatto problem to a father-and-son conflict, and for him the single all-important and transcending issue is rejection—personal rejection on the part of the father.

From "The Tragic Mulatto Theme in Six Works of Langston Hughes," *Five Black Writers*, ed. Donald B. Gibson (New York: New York University Press, 1970), 167–77. This excerpt is from 176.

Houston A. Baker, Jr.

Hughes may be more comprehensible within the framework of Afro-American verbal and musical *performance* than within the borrowed framework for the description of *written* inscriptions of cultural metaphor adduced by [Robert] Stepto [in *Afro-American Literature: The Reconstruction of Instruction*, 1979].

From *Blues, Ideology, and Afro-American Literature: A Vernacular Theory* (Chicago: University of Chicago Press, 1984), 97.

Steven C. Tracy

Oceola [in "The Blues I'm Playing"] demonstrates her brilliant technique in the classical idiom and even achieves some success in it, but ultimately rejects Mrs. Ellsworth's insistence on Oceola's sublimating her emotions in order to live life as it ought to be lived. The blues lyric, then is her emancipation proclamation, her break with attempts to "train" her too far away from her roots. . . .

. . . Hughes's exposure to the blues was fairly broad, but his own urban preference and his Harlem headquarters helped predispose him to vaudeville and professional blues, both of which were rooted in varying degrees in the folk-blues tradition. As a creative artist, Hughes was much like the blues composer or professional musician in seeking to draw on his folk roots not only out of pride and the need for individual artistic freedom but, sometimes, for economic reasons as well.

From *Langston Hughes and the Blues* (Chicago: University of Illinois Press, 1988), 122, 123.

Phillis R. Klotman

Inherent in Hughes's philosophy, throughout all of his works, in his recognition of, and pride in, the fact that the Afro-American has developed (or perhaps had innately) the ability to endure—to endure not only all of the sorrows to which man is heir, but also all of the racial calumnies devised by white society to defame its black citizens. Simple suggests that the assault of racism is comparable to the lethal attack of an atom bomb, but assures his friend Boyd that black people like him will be able to survive even such an attack.

From "Langston Hughes's Jesse B. Semple and the Blues," *Phylon: The Atlanta University Review of Race and Culture* 36, no. 1 (March 1975): 68–77. The excerpt is taken from 72.

Susan Blake

Hughes asks his audience to recognize their place in this [folk] tradition and use it as Simple uses the history stored up in his feet. . . . Modestly, like a relay runner, Langston Hughes picks up the folk tradition and carries it on toward the goal of social change in the real world.

From Susan L. Blake, "Old John In Harlem: The Urban Folktales of Langston Hughes," *Critical Essays on Langston Hughes*, ed. Edward J. Mullen (Boston: G.K. Hall, 1986), 167–75. This excerpt is taken from 172.

Edward Margolies

Hughes's short stories and sketches have in them something of the great ghetto writer, Sholem Aleichem. His characters, despite their defeats and humiliations, manage usually to survive and discover a sometimes bitter, sometimes ironic humor in their situations and the absurd circumstances that encumber them. In point of fact, Hughes's themes far transcend the deceptively simple narratives he writes; he writes really of the triumph of the human spirit over adversity. And he is rarely condescending or sentimental.

From *Native Sons: A Critical Study of Twentieth-Century Negro American Writers* (New York: J.B. Lippincott Company, 1968), 37.

James O. Young

With the exception of Langston Hughes's work, most of the fiction produced during the early 1930s continued to show the romantic influence of the Harlem Renaissance. None of these writers' [Fauset, Cullen, Thurman, McKay] works indicate that they had been influenced by the hard times.

From *Black Writers of the Thirties* (Baton Rouge: Louisiana State University Press, 1973), 205.

Mary Rohrberger

The realistic surfaces of Hughes's stories expose racism, social conditions, spiritual malaise; but beneath it all is the interior space of the black people themselves, Hughes' "soul world."

From "The Question of Regionalism: Limitation and Transcendence," *The American Short Story 1900–1945*, ed. Philip Stevick (Boston: Twayne, 1984), 158.

Jeffrey Walker

All the stores [in *Laughing* . . .] reveal Hughes's satiric attempts to reconcile the differences between races. His portraits mark him as one of the important writers of the postwar era.

From "Post-World War II Manners and Mores," *The American Short Story 1945–1980*, ed. Gordon Weaver (Boston: G.K. Hall, 1983), 33.

James Emanuel

During the Harlem Awakening of the 1920s, a lasting black American literary creed might have been born; but the requisite wary thoughtfulness and stern impulse to hoard and consolidate against a time of disaster were too infrequent. Langston Hughes laid the full groundwork by penetrating what he called his black "soul world" to an unprecedented and still unsurpassed degree; and his African themes combined with those of Claude McKay to forecast *negritude* beyond the Atlantic. Had a black aesthetic been formulated in the 1920s, it would probably have been free of individual restrictions and racial recriminations—echoing the very exuberance and geniality that made the Jazz Age incompatible with hardening creeds.

From "Blackness Can: A Quest For Aesthetics," *The Black Aesthetic*, ed. Addison Gayle, Jr. (New York: Anchor/Doubleday, 1972), 196–97. This excerpt taken from 196.

Hoyt Fuller

Langston Hughes kept that creed all his life, although he watched writers younger than himself abandon or reject it; and it must have been gratifying to him in his final years when he saw a new crop of black artists emerging upon the scene who, though ignorant of the credo, began to speak out in words very similar to his own. The young writers of the black revolution, at last, are able to do what the militant young writers of Langston Hughes's generation merely dreamed of.

From "The New Black Literature: Protest or Affirmation," *The Black Aesthetic*, ed. Addison Gayle, Jr. (New York: Anchor/Doubleday, 1972), 337.

Adam David Miller

Hughes, Wallace Thurman, and others found themselves castigated by that miniscule body of blacks who had successfully copied what they thought were white manners and habits and did not wish their shaky middle place to be disturbed by an awareness of those blacks they knew were "beneath" them. They were so put off by surfaces, that a few years later they were to reject Zora Neale Hurston's *Their Eyes Were Watching God* as a story of black migrant workers. . . . Fortunately for us, Hughes, Miss Hurston, and Arna Bontemps (*Black Thunder*) were not dissuaded by the indifferent or negative receptions, and as a result we have several works by writers who took the lives of their characters seriously, and rendered them with integrity, clarity, and precision.

From "Some Observations on a Black Aesthetic," *The Black Aesthetic*, ed. Addison Gayle, Jr. (New York: Anchor/Doubleday, 1972), 377.

Amiri Baraka

Hughes's importance, and the strength of his work, lies exactly in the fact that he reflects in his best work the lives and concerns of the black majority. . . . The fact that Hughes was aggressively focused on Black life and speech in his work whether accusingly or humorously or sadly or ecstatically so meant that his work would always be judged by bourgeois critics of whatever skin color as lightweight. As "Folksy."[3]

From "Langston Hughes," *Daggers and Javelins* (New York: Quill Books, 1984), 159, 161.

Notes

1. Sherwood Anderson, "Paying For Old Sins," *Nation* 139 (11 July 1934): 49–50, reprinted in *Critical Essays on Langston Hughes*, ed. Edward J. Mullen (Boston: G.K. Hall, 1986), 64–65. References are to the reprinted version. Hereafter cited in the text as Anderson.

2. Simple refers to the atom bomb in the story "Radioactive Redcaps," in *The Best of Simple*.

3. Baraka may overstate the extent to which even what he calls "bourgeois" critics see Hughes as lightweight; nonetheless, his essential point is extremely pertinent to an assessment of Hughes the story writer. For in Hughes's short fiction, two rare capacities converge: the capacity to use art consistently and successfully for social, political, and economic critique; and the capacity to use deceptively simple narratives—narratives inspired by the African-American folk or vernacular tradition, on the one hand, and by D. H. Lawrence's direct style on the other.

Moreover, Hughes's two main strengths (political acumen, folk simplicity) may sometimes misdirect readers. Certainly, these strengths are not at odds: a writer of political sophistication can certainly employ a simple narrative style; nevertheless, there may be times when the simplicity of style disguises the social critique too well, or when the social critique overwhelms the "technical" narrative improvisation.

When assessing Hughes the story writer, then, it is important to keep an eye on the ways he redefined the story for himself and the ways his stories went against the grain of other short-fiction modes in the twentieth century. His short fiction is substantial and original enough to influence the critical perspective by which it is assessed—to help determine, that is, the way we read his fiction.

Chronology

<table>
<tr><td>1902</td><td>James Langston Hughes born 1 February in Joplin, Missouri, to James Nathaniel and Carrie Mercer Langston Hughes.</td></tr>
<tr><td>1903–1915</td><td>Early on, often lives with his grandmother, Mary Sampson Patterson Leary Langston; Hughes lives in Buffalo; Cleveland; Lawrence, Kansas; Topeka; Colorado Springs; Kansas City, Kansas. In 1915, goes to Lincoln, Illinois, to live with his mother, her new husband (Homer Clark), and a half-brother named Kit. (Precisely when James and Carrie Hughes divorced is not known.)</td></tr>
<tr><td>1916</td><td>Begins writing poetry and is elected class poet of his grammar school class.</td></tr>
<tr><td>1916</td><td>The family moves to Cleveland, where Hughes attends Central High School and publishes poetry in the Belfry Owl, a school magazine. Starts to read Longfellow, Sandburg, Amy Lowell, and Edgar Lee Masters.</td></tr>
<tr><td>1918</td><td>Visits Chicago for the first time. Enjoys success as an athlete at Central High and begins to read philosophy, including Nietzsche and Schopenhauer.</td></tr>
<tr><td>1919</td><td>Spends summer in Mexico with his father; their relationship becomes severely strained.</td></tr>
<tr><td>1920</td><td>Graduates from Central High School in Cleveland.</td></tr>
<tr><td>1921</td><td>Teaches English in Mexico. In June publishes a poem, "The Negro Speaks of Rivers," in Crisis.</td></tr>
<tr><td>1921</td><td>Enrolls at Columbia University.</td></tr>
<tr><td>1922</td><td>Drops out in June.</td></tr>
<tr><td>1923</td><td>Lives in Harlem, works at a variety of jobs. Writes "The Weary Blues" and reads his poetry publicly for the first time. Meets Alain Locke and becomes part of what will be known as the Harlem Renaissance or the Harlem Awakening.</td></tr>
</table>

1923   Sails to West Africa as a cabin boy aboard the freighter *S. S. Malone*. Returns to the States, then sails to Holland.

1924   Sails again to Holland, resigns from the ship, and travels to Paris. Hears and sees black musicians perform in Paris and stays there almost a full year, returning to the States in December.

1925   Wins poetry prizes from *The Crisis* and *Opportunity*.

1926   Enrolls at Lincoln University and publishes *The Weary Blues*.

1927   Travels throughout the South on a reading tour. Meets Zora Neale Hurston. Publishes *Fine Clothes to The Jew*.

1928   Meets Mrs. Rufus Osgood Mason who becomes his patron.

1929   Graduates from Lincoln University.

1930   Breaks with his patron, Mrs. Mason.

1931   Receives Hammond Gold Award for *Not Without Laughter*. Tours the South again, giving readings. Meets Mary McLeod Bethune. Travels to Haiti with Zell Ingram. Travels to San Francisco as the guest of Noel Sullivan.

1932   Travels to the Soviet Union to work on an ill-fated film project. Is given a copy of *The Lovely Lady*, a collection of D. H. Lawrence's short stories, and is inspired to write short fiction.

1933   Travels extensively in the Soviet Union and Asia.

1934   *The Ways of White Folks* published. Participates in raising money for the defense of the Scottsboro Boys.

1934   His father dies. Hughes visits Mexico and remains for several months.

1935   Spends time in California. Hughes's play, *Mulatto*, produced in New York City. Works with Arna Bontemps on children's books.

1936   Six of his plays produced in Cleveland.

1937   Covers the Spanish Civil War for the *Baltimore African American*.

1940   Publishes his first autobiography, *The Big Sea*.

1943   Starts writing a column for the *Chicago Defender* and in the column invents the character Jesse B. Simple.

1950   *Simple Speaks His Mind* published.

1952   *Laughing To Keep From Crying* published.

1953   *Simple Takes A Wife* published. Hughes is interrogated by Senator Joseph McCarthy's anti-communist Congressional committee.

1955   *The First Book of Jazz* published.

1956   Hughes's second autobiography, *I Wonder As I Wander*, published.

1957   *Simple Stakes A Claim* published.

1959   *Selected Poems* published.

1961   *The Best of Simple* published.

1963   *Something In Common and Other Stories* published.

1967   *The Best Short Stories by Negro Writers*, edited by Hughes, and *The Panther and the Lash*, a book of poems, published. Hughes dies, 22 May, from complications following surgery.

Selected Bibliography

Primary Sources

Collections

The Best of Simple. New York: Hill and Wang, 1961. Includes "Feet Live Their Own Life," "Landladies," "Simple Prays a Prayer," "Conversation on the Corner," "Simple on Indian Blood," "A Toast to Harlem," "Simple and His Sins," "Temptation," "Wooing the Muse," "Vacation," "Letting Off Steam," "Jealousy," "Banquet in Honor," "A Veteran Falls," "High Bed," "Final Fear," "There Ought to Be a Law," "Income Tax," "No Alternative," "Springtime," "Last Whipping," "Seeing Double," "Simple on Military Integration," "Blue Evening," "A Letter from Baltimore," "Seven Rings," "What Can a Man Say?", "Empty Room," "Picture for Her Dresser," "Cocktail Sip," "Apple Strudel," "Bop," "Formals and Funerals," "Fancy Free," "Midsummer Madness," "Morals Is Her Middle Name," "They Come and They Go," "A Million—and One," "Two Loving Arms," "All in The Family," "Kick for Punt," "Subway to Jamaica," "No Tea for the Fever," "Boys, Birds, and Bees," "On the War- path," "A Hearty Amen," "Must Have a Seal," "Shadow of the Blues," "Once in a Wife-Time," "Present for Joyce," "Christmas Song," "Tied in A Bow," "Sometimes I Wonder," "Four Rings," "Simply Love," "Bang-Up End," "Duty Is Not Snooty," "Bones, Bombs, Chicken Necks," "A Dog Named Trilby," "Enter Cousin Minnie," "Radioactive Red Caps," "Two Sides Not Enough," "Puerto Ricans," "Minnie Again," "Vicious Circle," "Again Cousin Minnie," "Name in Print," "Minnie One More Time," "An Auto-Obituary," "Jazz, Jive, Jam."

Laughing to Keep from Crying. New York: Holt, 1952. Includes "Who's Passing for Who?", "Something in Common," "African Morning," "Pushcart Man," "Why, You Reckon?", "Saratoga Rain," "Spanish Blood," "Heaven to Hell," "Sailor Ashore," "Slice Him Down," "Tain't So," "One Friday Morning," "Professor," "Name in the Papers," "Powder-White Faces," "Rouge High," "On the Way Home," "Mysterious Madame Shanghai," "Never Room with a Couple," "Little Old Spy," "Tragedy at the Baths," "Trouble with Angels," "On the Road," "Big Meeting."

Simple Speaks His Mind. New York: Simon and Schuster, 1950. Includes "Feet Live Their Own Life," "Landladies," "Simple Prays a Prayer," "Conversation on the Corner," "Family Tree," "A Toast to Harlem," "Simple and His Sins," "Temptation," "Wooing the Muse," "Summer Ain't Simple," "A Word from 'Town & Country,'" "A Matter for a Book," "Surprise," "Vacation," "Letting Off Steam," "Jealousy," "Banquet in Honor," "After Hours," "High Bed," "Final Fear," "There Ought to Be a Law," "Income Tax," "No Alternative," "Question Period," "Lingerie," "Spring Time," "Last Whipping," "Nickel for a Phone," "Equality and Dogs," "Seeing Double," "Right Simple," "Ways and Means," "The Law," "Confused," "Something to Lean On," "In the Dark," "For the Sake of Argument," "Simple Pins on Medals," "A Ball of String," "Blue Evening," "When a Man Sees Red," "Race Relations," "Possum, Race, and Face," "A Letter from Baltimore."

Simple Stakes a Claim. New York: Rinehart, 1957. Includes "Simple's Platform," "Bang-Up Big End," "Big Round World," "Duty Is Not Snooty," "Great but Late," "Bones, Bombs, Chicken Necks," "A Dog Named Trilby," "Enter Cousin Minnie," "Radioactive Redcaps," "Face and Race," "Two Sides Not Enough," "Great Day," "With All Deliberate Speed," "Puerto Ricans," "Depression in the Cards," "The Atomic Age," "Minnie Again," "Sketch for TV," "Sex in Front," "Out-Loud Silent," "Color on the Brain," "New Kind of Dozens," "Vicious Circle," "Jim Crow's Funeral," "Again Cousin Minnie," "Cellophane Bandannas," "Negroes and Vacations," "Only Human," "Name in Print," "Golfing and Goofing," "Reason and Right," "Mississippi Fists," "Minnie One More Time," "Simple Stashes Back," "An Auto-Obituary," "Four-Way Celebrations," "Be Broad-Minded, Please!" "Grammar and Goodness," "Chips on the Shoulder," "Jazz, Jive, and Jam."

Simple Takes a Wife. New York: Simon and Schuster, 1953. Includes "Seven Rings," "What Can a Man Say?" "Empty Room," "Better Than a Pillow," "Explain That to Me," "Baltimore Womens," "Less Than a Damn," "Picture Her Dresser," "Cocktail Sip," "Apple Strudel," "Belles and Bells," "Bop," "A Hat Is a Woman," "Formals and Funerals," "Science Says It's a Lie," "Joyce Objects," "The Necessaries," "Second-Hand Clothes," "Fancy Free," "That Powerful Drop," "Never No More," "Simply Heavenly," "Midsummer Madness," "Morals Is Her Middle Name," "Party in The Bronx," "Last Thing at Night," "They Come and They Go," "A Million and One," "Two Loving Arms," "All in The Family," "Kick for Punt," "Night in Harlem," "Staggering Figures," "Tickets and Takers," "Subway to Jamaica," "No Tea for The Fever," "That Word Black," "Boys, Birds, Bees," "On The Warpath," "A Hearty Amen," "Colleges and Color," "Psychologies," "Must Have a Seal," "Shadow of The Blues," "Nothing but Roomers," "Here Comes Old Me," "Strictly for Charity," "Once in A Wife-Time," "Whiter Than Snow," "Simple Santa," "Present for Joyce," "Christmas Song," "Tied in a Bow," "Sometimes I

Wonder," "Dear Dr. Butts," "Castles in the Sand," "Four Rings," "Simply Love."

Simple's Uncle Sam. New York: Hill and Wang, 1965. Includes "Census," "Swinging High," "Contest," "Empty Houses," "The Blues," "God's Other Side," "Color Problems," "The Moon," "Domesticated," "Bomb Shelters," "Gospel Singers," "Nothing but A Dog," "Roots and Trees," "For President," "Atomic Dream," "Lost Wife," "Self-Protection," "Haircuts and Paris," "Adventure," "Minnie's Hype," "Yachts," "Ladyhood," "Coffee Break," "Lynn Clarisse," "Interview," "Simply Simple," "Golden Gate," "Junkies," "Dog Days," "Pose-Outs," "Soul Food," "Flay or Pray?", "Not Colored," "Cracker Prayer," "Rude Awakening," "Miss Boss," "Dr. Sidesaddle," "Wigs For Freedom," "Concernment," "Statutes and Statues," "American Dilemma," "Promulgations," "How Old Is Old?", "Weight in Gold," "Sympathy," "Uncle Sam."

Something in Common and Other Stories. New York: Hill and Wang, 1963. Includes "Thank You, Ma'am," "Little Dog," "Rock, Church," "Little Old Spy," "A Good Job Gone," "Who's Passing for Who?," "African Morning," "Pushcart Man," "Why, You Reckon?," "Saratoga Rain," "Spanish Blood," "Gumption," "Heaven to Hell," "Sailor Ashore," "Slice Him Down," "His Last Affair," "Tain't So," "Father and Son," "Professor," "Sorrow For Midget," "Powder-White Faces," "Rouge High," "The Gun," "Fine Accommodations," "No Place to Make Love," "On the Way Home," "Mysterious Madame Shanghai," "Patron of the Arts," "Early Autumn," "Never Room with a Couple," "Tragedy at The Baths," "Trouble with Angels," "On the Road," "Big Meeting," "Breakfast in Virginia," "Blessed Assurance," "Something in Common."

The Ways of White Folks. New York: Alfred Knopf, 1934. Includes "Cora Unashamed," "Slave on the Block," "Home," "Passing," "A Good Job Done," "Rejuvenation through Joy," "The Blues I'm Playing," "Red-Headed Baby," "Poor Little Black Fellow," "Little Dog," "Berry," "Mother and Child," "One Christmas Eve," "Father and Son."

Uncollected Stories

"Bodies in the Moonlight." *The Messenger*, April 1927, 105–6.

"Gold Piece." Brownie's Book, July 1921, 191–4. Reprinted in *Sadsa Encore*, Spring 1949, 30–32.

"In A Mexican City," *Brownie's Book*, April 1921, 102–5.

"The Little Virgin." *The Messenger*, November 1927, 327–8.

"Those Who Have No Turkey." *Brownie's Book*, November 1921, 324–6.

"The Young Glory of Him." *The Messenger*, June 1927, 177–8.

Books of Poetry, Published Plays, and a Novel

Ask Your Mama: Twelve Moods For Jazz. New York: Knopf, 1961. Poetry.

Dear Lovely Death. New York: Troutbeck Press, 1931. Poetry.

The Dream Keeper and Other Poems. New York: Knopf, 1932.

Fields of Wonder. New York: Knopf, 1947. Poetry.

Fine Clothes to The Jew. New York: Knopf, 1927. Poetry.

Five Plays of Langston Hughes. Bloomington: Indiana University Press, 1963.

Freedom's Plow. New York: Musette, 1943. Poetry.

Jim Crow's Last Stand. Atlanta: Negro Publication Society of America, 1943. Poetry.

Langston Hughes Reader. New York: Braziller, 1958. Selections from several genres.

Montage of a Dream Deferred. New York: Holt, 1951. Poetry.

Mule Bone: A Comedy of Negro Life. Written with Zora Neale Hurston. Edited with introductions by Geroge Houston Bass and Henry Louis Gates, Jr. New York: Harper Perennial, 1991. A play.

The Negro Mother and Other Dramatic Recitations. New York: Golden Stair Press, 1931.

Not Without Laughter. New York, Knopf, 1930. Novel.

One Way Ticket. New York: Knopf, 1949. Poetry.

The Panther And The Lash. New York: Knopf, 1967. Poetry. Reprinted in New York: Vintage, 1992.

Popo and Fifina. Written with Arna Bontemps. New York: Macmillan, 1932. Children's book.

Scottsboro Limited: Four Poems and a Play. New York: Golden Stair Press, 1932.

Selected Poems of Langston Hughes. New York: Knopf, 1959; Vintage, 1974.

Shakespeare in Harlem. New York: Knopf, 1942. Poetry.

Simply Heavenly. New York: Dramatists Play Service, 1959. Music by David Martin. Musical play.

Tambourines to Glory. New York: John Day, 1958. Play.

The Weary Blues. New York: Knopf, 1926. Poetry.

Plays Produced but Unpublished

(The dates are those of first productions.)

The Ballad of the Brown King. With music by Margaret Bonds. 1960.

The Barrier. With music by Jan Meyerowitz. 1950.

Black Nativity. 1961.

Don't You Want To Be Free. 1938.

Front Porch. 1938.

Esther. With music by Jan Meyerowitz. 1957.

Gospel Glow. 1962.

Jerico-Jim Crow. 1964.

Joy To My Soul. 1937.
Just Around The Corner. 1951.
Let Us Remember Him. 1963.
Little Ham. 1936.
Mulatto. 1935.
The Organizer. With music by James P. Johnson. 1939.
The Prodigal Son. 1965.
Soul Gone Home. 1937.
Street Scene. Lyrics. Book by Elmer Rice, music by Kurt Weill. 1947.
The Sun Do Move. 1942.
Troubled Island. 1936.
When Jack Hollers. Written with Arna Bontemps. 1936.

Nonfiction

Arna Bontemps-Langston Hughes Letters, 1925–1967. Edited by Charles Nichols. New York: Dodd, Mead, 1960.
The Big Sea: An Autobiography. New York: Knopf, 1940.
Black Magic: A Pictorial History of the American Negro in American Entertainment. Written with Milton Melzer. Englewood Cliffs, N.J.: Prentice Hall, 1967.
Black Misery. New York: Knopf, 1969.
Famous American Negroes. New York: Dodd, Mead, 1954.
Famous Negro Heroes of America. New York: Dodd, Mead, 1958.
Famous Negro Music Makers. New York: Dodd, Mead, 1955.
Fight For Freedom: The Story of the NAACP. New York: Norton, 1962.
The First Book of Africa. New York: Franklin Watts, 1960.
The First Book of Jazz. New York: Franklin Watts, 1955.
The First Book of Negroes. New York: Franklin Watts, 1952.
The First Book of Rhythms. New York: Franklin Watts, 1954.
Good Morning, Revolution: Uncollected Protest Writings by Langston Hughes. Edited by Faith Berry. New York: Lawrence Hill, 1973.
I Wonder As I Wander: An Autobiographical Journey. New York: Rinehart, 1956.
Pictorial History of the Negro In America. Written with Milton Melzer. New York: Crown, 1956; rev. eds. 1963, 1968. Revised as *A Pictorial History of Black Americans,* Written with Melzer and C. Eric Lincoln. New York: Crown, 1973.
The Sweet Flypaper of Life. New York: Simon and Schuster, 1955.

Secondary Sources

Biographies

Berry, Faith. *Langston Hughes: Before and Beyond Harlem.* Westport, Conn.: Lawrence Hill, 1983.
Dickinson, Donald C. *A Bio-Bibliography of Langston Hughes, 1902–1967.* Hamden, Conn.: Shoe String Press, 1967.

Haskins, James S. *Always Movin' On: The Life of Langston Hughes.* New York: Franklin Watts, 1976.

Quinot, Raymond. *Langston Hughes, ou L'Etoile Noire.* Brussels: Editions C.E.L.F., 1964.

Rampersad, Arnold. *The Life of Langston Hughes.* 2 vols. New York: Oxford University Press, 1986, 1988.

Rollins, Charlemae. *Black Troubadour: Langston Hughes.* Chicago: Rand McNally, 1970.

Critical Studies

Barksdale, Richard K. *Langston Hughes: The Poet And His Critics.* Chicago: American Library Association, 1977.

Bloom, Harold, editor. *Langston Hughes.* New York: Chelsea House, 1989.

Bruck, Peter. *The Black American Short Story in the Twentieth Century: A Collection of Critical Essays.* Amsterdam: Gruner, 1977.

Davis, Arthur P. *From the Dark Tower: Afro-American Writers From 1900–1960.* Washington, D.C.: Howard University Press, 1974.

Emanuel, James. *Langston Hughes.* New York: Twayne, 1967.

Gibson, Donald B. *Five Black Writers: Essays on Wright, Ellison, Baldwin, Hughes, and Leroi Jones.* New York: New York University Press, 1970.

Huggins, Nathan. *Harlem Renaissance.* New York: Oxford University Press, 1971.

Ikonne, Chidi. *From DuBois to Van Vechten: The Early New Negro Literature, 1903–1926.* Westport, Conn.: Greenwood Press, 1981.

Jemie, Onwuchekwa. *Langston Hughes: An Introduction to the Poetry.* New York: Columbia University Press, 1976.

Mandelik, Peter and Stanley Schatt. *Concordance to Langston Hughes.* Detroit: Gale Research, 1975.

Miller, R. Baxter. *The Art and Imagination of Langston Hughes.* Lexington: University of Kentucky Press, 1989.

Mullen, Edward, ed. *Critical Essays on Langston Hughes.* Boston: G. K. Hall, 1986.

O'Daniel, Therman B., ed. *Langston Hughes: Black Genius.* New York: Morrow, 1971.

Thurman, Wallace. *The Blacker the Berry.* New York: Collier Books, 1970.

Tracy, Steven C. *Langston Hughes and the Blues.* Chicago: University of Illinois Press, 1988.

Wintz, Cary D. *Black Culture and the Harlem Renaissance.* Houston: Rice University Press, 1988.

Young, James O. *Black Writers of the Thirties.* Baton Rouge: Louisiana State University Press, 1973.

Articles and Reviews

Ako, Edward O., "Langston Hughes and the Negritude Movement: A Study in Literary Influences." *College Language Association Journal* 28, no. 1 (September 1984): 46–56.

Anderson, Sherwood, "Paying For Old Sins." *Nation* 139 (11 July 1934): 49–50. Review of *The Ways of White Folks*.

Anon., "Langston Hughes and the Example of Simple." *Black World* 19, no. 8 (1970): 35–38.

Baldwin, James, "Sermons and Blues." *New York Times* (29 March 1959): 6.

Beyer, William, "Langston Hughes and Common Ground in the 1940s." *American Studies in Scandinavia* 23, no. 1 (1991), 29–42.

Blake, Susan L., "Old John in Harlem: The Urban Folktales of Langston Hughes." *Black American Literature Forum* 14 (1980): 100–4.

Bogumil, Mary L. and Michael R. Molino, "Pretext, Context, Subtext: Textual Power in the Writing of Langston Hughes, Richard Wright, and Martin Luther King, Jr." *College English* 52, no. 7 (November 1990), 800–11.

Bontemps, Arna, "Black and Bubbling." *Saturday Review of Literature* 35 (April 1952): 17. Review of *Laughing to Keep From Crying*.

Carey, Julian C., "Jesse B. Simple Revisited and Revised." *Phylon* 32 (1971): 158–63.

Cartey, Wilfred, "Four Shadows of Harlem." *Negro Digest* 18, no. 10 (1969): 22–25, 83–92.

Chandler, G. Lewis, "For Your Recreation and Reflection." *Phylon* 12 (Spring 1951): 94–95. Review of *Simple Speaks His Mind*.

Dandridge, Rita B., "The Black Woman as a Freedom Fighter in Langston Hughes's *Simple's Uncle Sam*." *College Language Association Journal* 18 (1974): 273–83.

Diakhate, Lamine, "Langston Hughes, Conquerat de l'espoir." *Presence Africaine* 64 (1967): 38–46.

Dodat, Francoise, "Situation de Langston Hughes." *Presence Africaine* 64 (1967): 47–50.

DuBois, W.E.B. and Alain Locke, "The Younger Literary Movement." *Crisis* 27 (1927): 161–63.

Emanuel, James Andrew, "The Short Stories of Langston Hughes." *Dissertation Abstracts* 27 (1966): 474A–575A.

Franke, Thomas L. "The Art of Verbal Performance: A Stylistic Analysis of Langston Hughes' 'Feet Live Their Own Life.'" *Language and Style* 19 (Fall 1986): 377–87.

Greene, Gita, "Remembering Langston Hughes: 'Langston Understood.'" *Langston Hughes Review* 5 (Spring 1986): 41–43.

Harper, Donna Akiba Sullivan, "'The Apple of His Eye': Du Bois on Hughes." *The Langston Hughes Review* 5, no. 2 (Fall 1986): 29–33.

Harper, Donna Akiba Sullivan, "The Complex Process of Crafting Langston Hughes's Simple, 1942–1949." *Dissertation Abstracts Index* 49 (December 1988): 1456A.

Hathaway, Heather, "'Maybe Freedom Lies in Hating': Miscegenation and the Oedipal Conflict." In *Refiguring the Father: New Feminist Readings of Patriarchy.* Edited by Patricia Yaeger, Beth Kowlaski-Wallace, and Nancy K. Miller. 153–67. Carbondale: University of Illinois Press, 1989. [Discusses Hughes's story, "Father and Son."]

Jackson, Blyden, "A Word About Simple." *College Language Association Journal* 11, no. 4 (1968): 310–18.

Jackson, Luther, [Untitled review of *Simple Stakes a Claim.*] *Crisis* 64 (May 1957): 576–77.

Joans, Ted, "A Memoir: The Langston Hughes I Knew." *Black World* 21, no. 11 (1972): 14–18.

Jones, Eldred, "Laughing To Keep From Crying: A Tribute To Langston Hughes." *Presence Africaine* 64 (1967): 51–55.

Kesteloot, Lilyan, "Negritude and Its American Sources." *Boston University Journal* 22, no. 2 (1974): 54–67.

Kitamura, Takao, "Langston Hughes and Japan." *Langston Hughes Review* 6 (1987): 8–12.

Klotman, Phillis, "Jesse B. Simple and the Narrative Art of Langston Hughes." *Journal of Narrative Technique* 3 (1973): 66–75.

Klotman, Phillis R., "Langston Hughes's Jesse B. Semple and the Blues." *Phylon* 36 (1975): 68–77.

Koprince, Susan, "Moon Imagery in *The Ways of White Folks. Langston Hughes Review* 1 (Spring 1983): 14–17.

Lee, Brian, "'Who's Passing for Who?' in the Fiction of Langston Hughes." In *Black Fiction: New Studies in the Afro-American Novel Since 1945*, 35–48. New York: Barnes & Noble, 1980.

Locke, Alain, [Untitled review of *The Ways of White Folks.*] *Survey Graphic* 23 (November 1934): 565.

Miller, Baxter R., "Langston Hughes and the 1980s: Rehumanization of Theory." *Black American Literature Forum* 15 (Fall 1981), 1–5.

Mintz, Lawrence E., "Langston Hughes's Jesse B. Simple: The Urban Negro as Wise Fool." *Satire Newsletter* 7 (1969): 11–21.

Moses, Wilson Jeremiah, "More Stately Mansions: New Negro Movements and Langston Hughes's Literary Theory." *Langston Hughes Review* 4 (Fall 1985): 40–46.

Mullen, Edward J., "The Literary Reputation of Langston Hughes In the Hispanic World." *Comparative Literature Studies* 13 (1976): 254–69.

Nifong, David Michael, "Narrative Technique and Theory in *The Ways of White Folks.*" *Black American Literature Forum* 15 (Fall 1981): 93–96.

Nower, Joyce, "Foolin' Master." *Satire Newsletter* 7 (1969): 5–10.

Presley, James, "The Birth of Jesse B. Simple." *Southwest Review* 58 (1973): 219–25.

Rampersad, Arnold, "Future Scholarly Projects on Langston Hughes." *Black American Literature Forum* 21 (Fall 1987): 305–16.

Redding, Saunders, "What It Means To Be Colored." *New York Times Book Review* (11 June 1950): 13. Review of *Simple Speaks His Mind.*

Ricks, Sybil Ray, "A Textual Comparison of Langston Hughes's 'Mulatto,' 'Father and Son,' and 'The Barrier.'" *Black American Literature Forum* 15, no. 3 (Fall 1981), 101–3.

Story, Ralph D., "Patronage and the Harlem Renaissance: You Get What You Pay For." *College Language Association Journal* 32, no. 3 (March 1989), 284–85.

Tracy, Steven C., "Simple's Great African-American Joke." *College Language Association Journal* 27 (March 1984): 239–53.

Van Vechten, Carl, "Dialogues But Barbed." *New York Times Book Review* (7 May 1950): 10. Review of *Simple Speaks His Mind.*

Van Vechten, Carl, "In The Heart of Harlem." *New York Times* (31 May 1953): 5. Review of *Simple Takes a Wife.*

Walker, Alice, "Turning Into Love; Some Thoughts on Surviving and Meeting Langston Hughes." *Callaloo: An Afro-American and African Journal of Arts and Letters* 12, no. 4 (Fall 1989), 663–66.

Williams, Melvin G., "The Gospel According to Simple." *Black American Literature Forum* 11 (1977): 46–48.

Williams, Melvin G., "Langston Hughes's Jesse B. Simple: A Black Walter Mitty." *Negro American Literature Forum* 10 (1976): 66–69.

Bibliographies

Bassett, John E. *Harlem in Review: Critical Reactions to Black American Writers, 1917–1939.* London and Toronto: Associated University Presses, 1992. [Includes annotated bibliographies of reviews of Hughes's *The Ways of White Folks, The Weary Blues,* and *The Big Sea.*]

Dickinson, Donald C. *A Bio-Bibliography of Langston Hughes, 1902–1967.* Hamden, Conn.: Arcon Books, 1967. Rev. ed., 1972.

Miller, R. Baxter. *Langston Hughes and Gwendolyn Brooks: A Reference Guide.* Boston: G.K. Hall, 1978.

O'Daniel, Therman B., "Langston Hughes: A Selected Classified Bibliography." *College Language Association Journal* 11, no. 4 (1968): 349–66.

Index

Aleichem, Sholem, 98
Algren, Nelson, 74
Anderson, Judith, 75
Anderson, Marian, 75
Anderson, Sherwood, 3, 56,
    83–84
Arden, Elsie, 75

Baker, Houston A., Jr., 7, 94
Baldwin, James, 13, 43, 55, 60, 71
Baraka, Amiri, 105, 106n3
Bass, George Houston, 73
Bender, Albert, 75
Bergman, Ingrid, 27
Blake, Susan, 97
Bojangles, Mr., 72
Bontemps, Arna, 76, 86, 104
Brooklyn Daily Eagle, 62
Buck, Pearl S., 77

Césaire, Aimé, 78
Chekhov, Anton, 9
Chicago Defender, The, 31, 34, 37,
    39, 62, 88
Cooper, J. California, 61
Cullen, Countee, 89, 99

Davis, Arthur P., 93
de la Cabada, Juan, 76
Denby, William, 71
Dickens, Charles, 9, 58
Dos Passos, John, 5
Dove, Rita, 61

Ellington, Duke, 75
Ellison, Ralph, 30, 43, 60, 71
Emanuel, James, 4, 43, 102
Esquire, 75

Faulkner, William, 16, 45, 55
Fauset, Jessie, 99
Field, Sara Bard, 75
Fiske, Dwight, 75
Fuller, Hoyt, 103

Gaines, Ernest J., 61
Gates, Henry Louis, Jr., 7, 73
Guillen, Nicolas, 78

Hayes, Roland, 75, 77
Hemingway, Ernest, 3, 18, 22, 56,
    59
Himes, Chester, 71
Hughes, Langston: and Africa, 4;
    and the black aesthetic, 62,
    69, 83, 91, 103, 105; and the
    blues, 15, 38, 62, 74, 94–96;
    and character type, 51–56;
    and the Civil Rights Move-
    ment, 39–41; and the Cotton
    Club, 71; and "the dozens,"
    7, 62; and folktales/folk tradi-
    tion, 44, 97, 105; and the
    Great Depression, 5, 49, 52;
    and Harlem/Harlem Renais-
    sance, 20, 35, 49, 71–72, 74,
    83, 89, 99; and jazz, 15, 52,

119

54, 62, 74, 94, 102; and Jim
Crow laws, 34, 38–39, 48,
71–72, 77; and lynching, 11–
12, 16; and Marxism, 5, 17,
28, 91, 105; and modernism,
5, 61; and the mulatto, figure
of in Hughes's short fiction,
56, 93; and narrative modes,
4, 56–59, 100; and negritude,
62, 102; and Paris, 13–14;
and religion, 15; and Russia,
6, 73–74; and Scottsboro
trial, 16; and satire, 101;
and the Spanish civil war,
76–77; and Uncle John, 44;
and women characters,
35–37

AUTOBIOGRAPHIES
Big Sea, The, 27, 33, 71–73
I Wonder As I Wander, 27, 33,
73–77

DRAMA
Mule Bone, 72–73

ESSAYS AND SPEECHES
"Negro Artist and the Racial
Mountain, The," 3, 38, 43,
58, 62, 69–71
"My America," 77–78
"Who Is Simple?", 31–33
"Writer's Position in America,
The," 70–71

MOTION PICTURE
"Black and White," 6

NOVEL
Not Without Laughter, 90

POETRY
"Ask Your Mama," 6
Weary Blues, The, 5

SHORT FICTION
"Adventure," 38
"American Dilemma," 41
"African Morning," 21, 52, 57
"Berry," 15, 92
Best of Simple, The, 31, 39
"Big Meeting," 28
"Blessed Assurance," 49
"Blues, The," 38, 95
"Blues I'm Playing, The," 14–
15, 54–57
"Bodies in the Moonlight," 4
"Breakfast in Virginia," 48
"Cora Unashamed," 6, 8–10,
15, 57, 74
"Duty Is Not Snooty," 39
"Early Autumn," 46
"Father and Son," 14, 16–17,
55, 57, 92
"Feet Live Their Own Life,"
35, 53
"Fine Accomodations," 48
"Good Job Gone, A," 7, 75
"Gumption," 48
"Gun, The," 44–45
"Heaven To Hell," 22
"His Last Affair," 46–47
"Home," 11–12, 52, 57, 70–71
"Jazz, Jive, and Jam," 37
"Jealousy," 36
Laughing To Keep From Crying,
16, 19–30, 58, 75, 86, 101
"Little Old Spy," 27, 58
"Mother and Child," 14–16
"Mysterious Madame Shang-
hai," 27, 58

"Name In The Papers," 25, 58
"On The Road," 28–29, 53, 75
"On The Way Home," 26
"One Friday Morning," 24–25
"Passing," 11–12, 54
"Poor Little Black Fellow," 6,
    13–14
"Powder-White Faces," 26
"Pushcart Man," 25, 58
"Red-Headed Baby," 13, 52
"Rejuvenation through Joy,"
    12, 27, 57
"Rock, Church," 49
"Rouge High," 26
"Sailor Ashore," 22
"Saratoga Morning," 22, 57
"Seven Rings, The," 40
Simple Speaks His Mind, 19, 35–
    36, 87
Simple Stakes A Claim, 88
Simple Takes A Wife, 87
"Slave on the Block," 6, 10–
    11, 14
"Slice Him Down," 22
"Something In Common," 21,
    57
Something In Common, 31,
    44–50
"Sorrow For A Midget," 45–46
"Spanish Blood," 22
"Summer Ain't Simple," 36
"Tain't So," 23–24
"Toast to Harlem, A," 40
"Trouble With Angels, The," 27
Ways of White Folks, The, 3–18,
    52, 54, 61–62, 71, 75, 83–85,
    90
"Who's Passing For Who?",
    20–21, 57
"Why, You Reckon?", 25

Hurston, Zora Neale, 13, 58, 72–
    73, 104

Iduarte, Andres, 76
Iturbi, Jose, 75

Jackson, Blyden, 44
Jackson, Luther, 88
James, Henry, 84
Jeffers, Robinson, 75
Jemie, Onwuchekwa, 91
Johnson, J.C., 74
Johnson, J.P., 74
Joyce, James, 3, 18, 58

Kafka, Franz, 45
Kirchwey, Frida, 69
Kenan, Randall, 61
King, Rev. Martin Luther, Jr., 71
Krishnamuri, 75

Lawrence, D. H., 5, 17–18, 42,
    51, 57, 61, 73–74, 84
Lewis, Sinclair, 5
Locke, Alain, 85
Louis, Joe, 76

Mabley, Jackie, 88
McCullers, Carson: "Ballad of the
    Sad Cafe, The," 74
McKay, Claude, 60, 99, 102
Malraux, André, 76
Mansfield, Katherine, 18, 56, 83
Margolies, Edward, 98
Mason, Charlotte, 6, 14, 17
Miller, Adam David, 104
Miller, Loren, 74
Miller, R. Baxter, 16, 92
Morrison, Toni, 60
Motley, Willard, 71

Nation, The, 69, 83
Neruda, Pablo, 76
New Yorker, The, 25, 62
Nifong, David, 4

O'Connor, Frank, 83
Ostendorf, Berndt, 8

Partisan Review, The, 61
Porter, Katherine Anne, 3, 83
Prevert, Jacques, 74

Rampersad, Arnold, 6, 31, 34, 42,
    69, 78, 90
Reed, Ishmael
Robeson, Paul, 77
Rohrberger, Mary, 100
Roosevelt, Franklin, 77

Sandburg, Carl, 42
Saroyan, William, 75
Schuyler, George, 5, 69, 88

Senghor, Leopold Sedar, 78
Steffens, Lincoln, 75
Stepto, Robert, 94
Sullivan, Noel, 75

Thurman, Wallace, 5, 72, 99, 104
Tolson, Melvin B., 89
Till, Emmett, 71
Tracy, Steven C., 95

Van Vechten, Carl, 87

Walker, Alice, 60–61
Walker, Jeffrey, 101
Wallace, Henry, 77
Welch, Marie, 57
Wilkie, Wendell, 77
Wright, Richard, 14, 60, 71

Yerby, Frank, 71
Young, James O., 99

The Author

Hans Ostrom is an associate professor of English at the University of Puget Sound. He earned his Ph.D. from the University of California, Davis and has taught at Johannes Gutenberg University in Mainz, Germany. His publications include *Three to Get Ready*, a novel, and *Lives and Moments: An Introduction to Short Fiction*. With Wendy Bishop, he is coeditor of *Colors of a Different Horse*, a collection of essays about the theory and practice of teaching creative writing. His scholarly interests include the short story, verse satire, British romanticism, and the Harlem Renaissance.

The Editor

General Editor Gordon Weaver earned his B.A. in English at the University of Wisconsin-Milwaukee in 1961; his M.A. in English at the University of Illinois, where he studied as a Woodrow Wilson Fellow, in 1962; and his Ph.D. in English and creative writing at the University of Denver in 1970. He is author of several novels, including *Count a Lonely Cadence, Give Him a Stone, Circling Byzantium*, and most recently *The Eight Corners of the World* (1988). Many of his numerous short stories are collected in *The Entombed Man of Thule, Such Waltzing Was Not Easy, Getting Serious, Morality Play, A World Quite Round*, and *Men Who Would Be Good* (1991). Recognition of his fiction includes the St. Lawrence Award of Fiction (1973), two National Endowment for the Arts Fellowships (1974, 1989), and the O. Henry First Prize (1979). He edited *The American Short Story, 1945–1980: A Critical History*, and is currently editor of *Cimarron Review*. He is professor of English at Oklahoma State University. Married, and the father of three daughters, he lives in Stillwater, Oklahoma.